MERCHANTS OF MADNESS

John —

With best wishes,

24.02.09

MERCHANTS OF MADNESS

THE METHAMPHETAMINE EXPLOSION
IN THE GOLDEN TRIANGLE

BERTIL LINTNER AND MICHAEL BLACK

SILKWORM BOOKS

ISBN: 978-974-9511-59-6

Published in 2009 by
Silkworm Books
6 Sukkasem Road, T. Suthep
Chiang Mai 50200, Thailand
info@silkwormbooks.com
www.silkwormbooks.com

Typeset by Silk Type in Minion Pro 10 pt.
Cover design by Trasvin Jittidecharak, artwork by Umaporn Soetphannuek
Printed in Thailand by O.S. Printing House, Bangkok

10 9 8 7 6 5 4 3 2 1

CONTENTS

LIST OF ILLUSTRATIONS

Maps

Color Plates (between pages 60 and 61)

Black-and-White Plates

INTRODUCTION AND
ACKNOWLEDGMENTS

FOR DECADES, Southeast Asia's Golden Triangle—where the borders of Thailand, Laos, and Burma intersect—has been infamous for its opium production. Small quantities of raw opium were smoked locally, while the derivative heroin was smuggled to markets in Southeast Asia, Australia, North America, and Europe. In the 1990s more than two thousand tons of raw opium was harvested annually. As it takes ten kilograms of raw opium plus precursor chemicals to make one kilogram of heroin, that was enough of the narcotic to feed the world's addict population several times over.

But then, in recent years, international drug agencies began to announce significant steps towards the elimination of opium production in the Burmese sector of the Golden Triangle, where most of the region's poppies have always been grown. A success story? Hardly. In regards to the quantities being harvested, the production is merely back to what it was before the opium boom of the 1990s. Opium production is down in some areas along the Chinese border—while it has increased in other parts of northern and northeastern Burma.

More importantly, in the 1990s the drug gangs in the Golden Triangle began to produce methamphetamine, a synthetic drug that does not depend on any unreliable crop such as the opium poppy. By the end of the decade, methamphetamine production has become a more lucrative source of income for the gangs than opium and heroin had ever been.

In Thailand the drug has become known as *yaba*, "madness drug" or "madness medicine." And it is an even more serious threat to society than heroin ever was, as the consumers are not only "traditional" drug users—young men and some women in the slums of Bangkok, juvenile delinquents, and other outcasts—but also high school and university students, workers in factories and on construction sites, long-distance bus and truck drivers, and ordinary partygoers. Millions of people across Thailand have become regular or occasional users. And, unlike heroin, *yaba* has successfully transcended socioeconomic barriers, creating a new wave of drug addiction on an unprecedented scale in Thailand.

Unlike heroin, which is a "downer," *yaba*—or speed—is an "upper" that makes those who take it hyperactive and often aggressive. It has led to murders, stabbings, and the kidnapping of innocent people. And it has broken down the users mentally as well as physically. It is a real "madness drug."

But who are the merchants of this madness—the ones who produce and sell this scourge to society, and who are willing to sacrifice the well-being of the region's young people for personal profits? The aim of this book is to explain who they are and how they became the new drug lords of the Golden Triangle. But it is impossible to understand the drug problem in Burma without analyzing the historical, political, and ethnic problems that caused it in the first place. The drug trade is not a criminal activity comparable with burglary, muggings, or murder. It is the outcome of several decades of ethnic and political conflicts in Burma along with the inability of successive military regimes in that country to find solutions to its decades-long internal strife.

Bertil Lintner, a journalist and author based in Chiang Mai in northern Thailand, has covered the Golden Triangle drug trade for more than two decades and traveled extensively in the drug producing areas. He is the author of *Burma in Revolt: Opium and Insurgency since 1948*, a detailed study of the tragic events that have led to today's massive drug production in the Golden Triangle. He has also written other books about Burma, and has examined the drug trade and related issues in numerous articles and seminar papers that have garnered respect from academics as well as governments. From 1982 to 2004 he covered Burma for the now defunct Hong Kong weekly *Far Eastern Economic Review*.

Michael Black is a Thailand-based freelance writer who has also written extensively about the region's drug trade for *Jane's Intelligence Review* and other prestigious publications. He has lived in the area since 2002, researching the region's vice economy and the nexus between the informal world and formal governance. He has traveled extensively in the region and interviewed several players in the Golden Triangle drug trade. These include sources close to drug production facilities, traffickers, money launderers, financiers, and other elements within the secretive world of the Golden Triangle's colorful milieu of narco-militias and complex array of drug operators.

This book is based on that extensive research, spanning several decades and including a collection of firsthand accounts of the drug trade from law enforcement officers and intelligence officials alike, as well as sources close to the drug traffickers themselves. It is our hope that this book will lead to a better understanding of the Golden Triangle drug trade, how it all began, and how it has grown to become a multi-billion dollar criminal enterprise.

But we also look at possible solutions to the problem and offer views that differ from the conventional approach to the drug trade, which tend to ignore the underlying ethnic and political issues that created the trade in the first place. We believe that policies so far have been not only ineffective but outright counterproductive. Few, if any, international "drug experts" have paid much attention to the root causes of the problem: Burma's ethnic conflicts, and decades of stifling military rule. Without a lasting solution to these issues Burma will remain a source of political despair— and drugs from the Golden Triangle will continue to flood the markets of the region and the world.

This book would not have been possible without the assistance of numerous sources in the area. Most of them have to remain anonymous, but we can name US academic and researcher Alfred W. McCoy as a source of tremendous inspiration. His groundbreaking study, *The Politics of Heroin in Southeast Asia*, was first published in the early 1970s but, in essence, its findings and conclusions still remain valid. Drug production, regional politics, insurgency, and counterinsurgency are all interrelated. We are also grateful to people living in the drug-producing areas who were willing to talk openly about the trade and the merchants who control it. Facts were checked with them and with drug enforcement officials, who read parts of the manuscript, offered useful criticism, and provided additional information. Finally, we would like to thank our old friend Edward Loxton for proofreading the manuscript and tidying up our English.

Chiang Mai, Thailand, October 2008

FIGURE 1. Map of Burma

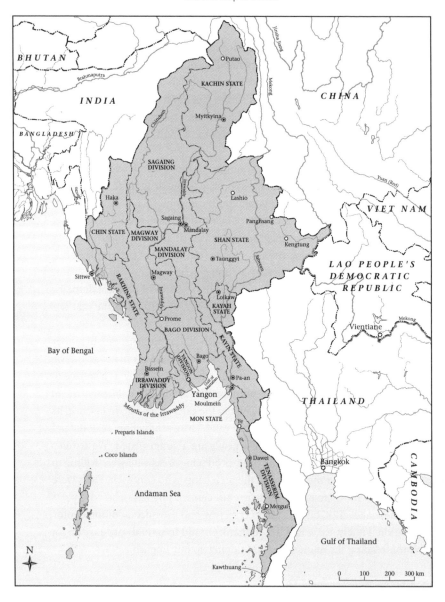

ONE

THE MADNESS

Reuters/Profile

IT WAS a scene that the people in Bangkok who witnessed it found hard to forget. Paitoon Puthiporn, a twenty-nine-year-old drug-crazed man with blood streaming down his face, was holding a knife to the throat of a young female student, Patcharaphant Jiravanich. Having cut himself in a rage, he had for no apparent reason taken nineteen-year-old Patcharaphant hostage. Paitoon's eyes were rolled back, his pupils obscured by his eyelids. High on speed, he evidently had no idea what he was doing. The young woman stood there motionless with her eyes closed, not knowing what to expect. A crowd gathered below the balcony on which they were standing. Then a plainclothes police officer, pretending to be a doctor, climbed a ladder leaning against the balcony and began negotiating with Paitoon. To the relief of the onlookers, the crazed drug addict released Patcharaphant inside the house, where police took him into custody.

It was August 2002, and far from the first time such a hostage-taking had occurred in Bangkok. The English-language Thai daily *Bangkok Post* had already, in October 1996, published a strikingly similar picture of a young man who had cut himself in the throat to deter police after he had held his wife hostage for three hours. On another occasion, an addict held hostage a five-year-old. Desperate to avoid the repeat of a similar incident in which a child was hacked to death by a delusional user, the police shot the man dead.

Drug abuse is not new to Thailand; opium was smoked more than a hundred years ago in dens in Bangkok's Chinatown, and, more recently, in hilltribe villages in the northern mountains. Then heroin, a much more powerful derivative of opium, became the drug of choice in the 1970s and 1980s.

Raw opium was collected from poppy plants in the Golden Triangle, with the bulk of the production taking place in Burma. The laboratories where the opium was refined into white powder (heroin) were also located in Burma, while the financing of the operations, and the trade itself, took place mostly through Thailand.

In the 1990s, however, heroin gradually ceased to be such a big problem. Young and not-so-young addicts alike turned to methamphetamine tablets, which were much cheaper and more readily available. Pushers sold them first in the slums of Bangkok and in the backstreets of Chiang Mai—and before long in towns all over the country. Until then, methamphetamines had been known in Thailand as *yama*, or horse drug. When it first showed up, in the mid-1950s, it was sold at gas stations, where truck drivers would pop a pill to stay alert on long-distance journeys. College students would also take it to stay awake before exams. As "uppers," methamphetamines give extra strength and energy to those who take them.

But in July 1996 Thai government spokesman Somsak Prisananananthakul announced that from then on methamphetamines would be referred to as *yaba*, or "madness drug." The name *yama* gave the impression that it would enable users "to work tirelessly like a horse," Somsak stated. By calling it *yaba* the Thai authorities hoped to give a more accurate description of the drug's harmful effects. And, as Paitoon Puthiporn and others showed, it really did turn people mad.

In September 1996 the then secretary-general of Thailand's Office of Narcotics Control Board (ONCB), Preecha Champarat, said that methamphetamines posed a greater threat than other drugs such as heroin. "Unlike heroin, most youths take it for fun without having second thoughts about its effect or their health," Preecha told a seminar in Bangkok. He also said that there were 247,965 registered addicts nationwide in 1993–1994, "but the real number was higher and the addiction rate was rising."

In most countries, methamphetamines usually come in powder form, allowing users to snort it through their nostrils or inhale the fumes when heated. The pill version, which is more common in Southeast Asia, can either be popped, or heated and then inhaled. Either way, the effects on the user are devastating. Apart from making people stay awake, methamphetamines cause hallucinations and severe dehydration. They also increase the heart rate, make people paranoid, and, when the effects are wearing off, often lead to depression. Suicides are not uncommon.

In May 2000 the ONCB's General Watcharapol Prasarnrajkit described the production, trafficking, and consumption of illegal drugs—especially methamphetamines—as "the most dangerous problem" facing not only Thailand but also the rest of Southeast Asia. The users now were not only long-distance truck drivers and college students but people from all walks of life. It had become a national scourge.

In 1997, about twenty-two million speed pills were seized in Thailand. That figure rose to thirty million in 1998 and almost forty million in 1999. A record number of 95.9 million pills were seized in 2002. In that year the street price of a pill was 120 baht, or about the same as a couple of bottles of beer. While heroin had a market in Thailand, really high prices could be fetched when the drug was smuggled overseas to North America, Europe, and Australia. But that involved an elaborate network of couriers, financiers, and professional smugglers. The main market for *yaba* was—and still is—in Thailand, where there is a quicker return for the money and much less risk, since the drug does not have to be smuggled out through Thai ports and airports. Different types of methamphetamines are also much easier to manufacture than heroin. The quantities of chemical precursors that are needed to produce a synthetic drug are considerably less than the quantities of raw material required to produce a plant-based drug such as heroin. In the early 1990s, *yaba* became a booming business in Thailand, reaching a far wider clientele than heroin ever had.

"Businesswise, heroin traffickers have now turned to amphetamines because of the immense profits they bring," Lieutenant General Noppadol Soomboonsap, head of the Police Narcotics Suppression Bureau, told the *Bangkok Post* in March 1997. Each tablet cost less than ten baht (about thirty US cents) to produce, while street dealers would pay two or three times that price to the distributors. But individual street dealers would not be able to sell many pills, so the huge profits were reaped by the producers and distributors.

The shift from heroin to methamphetamines is also reflected in official statistics for drug-related arrests in Thailand. In 1990, 62.2 percent of drug offenders were indicted for crimes related to cannabis, while 21.3 percent of the cases were heroin-related and only 3.7 percent connected to methamphetamines, while in the year 2000 cannabis-related charges accounted for only 9.5 percent of indictments, and those related to heroin and methamphetamines accounted for 2.2 percent and 79.5 percent respectively. But that has not deterred people from buying, selling, and consuming *yaba*. In 1997, Sorasit Sangprasert of the ONCB stated, "*yaba* is now in every province. Some teachers and students have been found to sell *yaba*."

Dao, a thirty-two-year-old woman in the northern Thai city of Chiang Mai says she takes one or two *yaba* pills a day to give her a lift—and because she works in a factory and wants some extra energy. She has used *yaba* for about a decade and buys the pills from a fellow worker at the factory. Somchai, a twenty-one-year-old student in Chiang Mai, buys his *yaba* pills from a fellow student at one of the city's universities. He heats the pills and inhales the fumes in his dormitory together with friends, who are also users. They can stay awake for more than twenty-four hours—but then have to sleep for twenty. Chart, who is now twenty-four, has taken *yaba* pills since he was fourteen and buys them in a hilltribe village north of Chiang Mai.

Many users have also become dealers to finance their habit—and some belong to Chiang Mai's infamous youth gangs. Violence and turf wars between rival gangs have been a social problem in Chiang Mai for decades, along with prostitution, HIV/AIDS—and drugs. Chiang Mai is a frontier town that has always had a large transient population as many young people migrate to or through the city from the surrounding countryside as well as neighboring Burma, Laos, and China. Many hilltribe people in the area are stateless. The gangs give these youths a sense of belonging. Various gangs may clash, but there is a strong feeling of brotherhood among the members of the same group. And Chiang Mai is close to the Golden Triangle, one of the world's oldest and biggest drug-producing areas for first opium and heroin and now methamphetamines.

Both boys and girls, some barely in their teens, also sell sexual services for as little as three hundred baht (about US$8.50) to buy alcohol, glue to sniff—and *yaba*. The biggest and most vicious of the gangs in Chiang Mai are the Samurais, who earned that nickname because they are often seen wielding long swords while riding motorcycles at high speed through the city after dark. The Samurais have several hundred members and can be seen at night on the ring-roads that encircle Chiang Mai.

Another prominent gang is called Ya Kha, named after a thatched-roof motorcycle repair shed, while the Set Den got their name because they were "left over," or social outcasts. Among those formed after 2000, the Bin Laden gang gained notoriety when it was involved in the murder of members of rival gangs. The name Bin Laden was taken to evoke an image of violence and daring attacks.

There are also all-girl gangs in Chiang Mai, of which the Vampires are the biggest, with 180 members. "They like to sleep with as many boys as they can, and I can't prevent them from doing that, but at the very least I can teach them about safe sex," says Laddawan Chaininpun, an older woman who has worked with the youth gangs for more than a decade. She realizes that she cannot change their behavior completely but, by bringing them together for football matches and similar events, she has managed to reduce the level of gang-related violence in the city. She is also telling them to stay off drugs, and not only because they harm themselves by taking *yaba*. The street gangs are on the lowest—and therefore the most vulnerable—level in the drug hierarchy, which begins with the drug lords in the Golden Triangle and includes powerful business interests in the region. They, not the Samurais or other gangs, earn huge profits from the trade, while the young dealers hardly make enough to pay for their own habits.

But it was the street dealers and petty traders who became the main targets when former prime minister Thaksin Shinawatra on February 1, 2003, launched a nationwide "war on drugs." The scourge had got out of hand, and the authorities had decided to take stern measures against it. Too harsh, however, critics argued.

When the campaign ended towards the end of that year, 2,598 people had been killed, and the majority of deaths occurred in northern Thailand. The authorities said that this was mainly the outcome of intergang warfare, while human rights organizations asserted that the dead were victims of extrajudicial killings by the police. Certainly, by no means had all of them had anything to do with drugs. Human Rights Watch stated in a 2004 report that "Throughout the war on drugs, the Thai government at the highest levels encouraged violence and discrimination against anyone suspected of using or trafficking narcotic drugs. At the outset of the war on drugs, Prime Minister Thaksin sought to distinguish between drug users, who he said should be treated as 'victims' and 'patients,' and drug traffickers, who were to be harshly punished. In practice, drug users along with drug traffickers became the targets of state-sponsored killings and ill-treatment."

Meryam Dabhoiwala, a researcher with the Hong Kong-based NGO the Asian Legal Resource Center, wrote after the extremely violent 2003 campaign: "Among those killed were persons who had voluntarily joined police reform programs, in many cases months before the drug war began. One of them was Jamnian Nualwilai, a former drug peddler in Muang (central) district of Ratchaburi, on February 13. His wife believes the police killed him and blamed it on his old drug gang. Jamnian had joined a reform program two years ago, and sent in his urine every month to prove he was still clean. Five days before the killing, police commended Jamnian for his conduct and told him his name would be removed from the blacklist. 'I had not the slightest idea that the delisting would end up with my husband being shot dead,' his wife Kik said."

According to Dabhoiwala, many people were also killed after going to the police station in response to having their names blacklisted. Boonyung Tangtong was one of ten persons in his neighborhood killed after surrendering to the police. Dabhoiwala quoted Boonyung's sixteen-year-old son Adirek as saying that before being shot in his own home his father had reported to the nearest police station. Adirek was certain the police killed his father.

In Chiang Rai, north of Chiang Mai, police reportedly even put their informers in jail after they found it difficult to meet government targets for arrests. Officials had to scramble to fill new government quotas or risk losing their jobs. On February 15 the Thai interior minister was reported as having voiced his displeasure at certain provinces that were not meeting their quotas, warning that they would be assessed on February 19 and at that date sacked, transferred, or demoted.

According to Dabhoiwala, the first child to be killed was a nine-year-old boy, Chakraphan Srisa-ard, who was shot on February 23 when police fired at the car carrying him and his mother. His father had already been arrested. Dabhoiwala wrote that one of the boy's uncles had stated, "The police kept shooting and shooting at the car. They wanted them to die. Even a child was not spared." The next child to be killed was a sixteen-month-old baby, shot in her mother's arms by an "unknown gunman" on February 26. A hilltribe couple was shot dead on February 24 on suspicion of selling drugs, Dabhoiwala asserted. Their three children, the youngest of whom was a six-year-old girl, were left orphaned. Since then, no evidence has been found to suggest the couple had any drug dealings. According to relatives quoted by Dabhoiwala, they "had to die to help make the state suppression records look good."

The controversial "war on drugs" nevertheless caused a dent in the trade. Seizures in 2003 dropped to 71.5 million pills, another sharp drop followed in 2004 with 31.1 million pills seized, and in 2005 only 15.4 million pills were interdicted. But the trend was temporary—and the big drug lords were never really affected. They found new markets in Laos, Cambodia, and Vietnam, and before long *yaba* was also back on the streets of Bangkok, Chiang Mai, and other Thai cities. In June 2008 the police in northern Thailand noted that drug smuggling was increasing in the area. The *Bangkok Post* reported that "the narcotics market is bustling as unfavorable economic conditions, particularly inflation, have driven a number of new sellers into the illegal business since early this year."

There seems to be no end to the problem, and, having successfully eradicated opium in its own mountains, Thailand now has to live with *yaba* abuse of a magnitude that surpasses the harm that heroin addiction ever did to society.

WHAT ARE METHAMPHETAMINES?

Amphetamine was first synthesized in 1887 by a German chemist, Lazar Edeleanu, from a series of compounds related to the derivative of the ephedra plant. The compounds, called ephedrine, were also used to synthesize the related drug methamphetamine, which was first produced in Japan in 1918 by chemist Akira Ogata. Both amphetamines and methamphetamines were later produced chemically, but it was not until 1929 that pharmacological uses were found for the new drugs. Amphetamine was first marketed in the 1930s as Benzedrine in an over-the-counter inhaler to treat nasal congestion. By 1937 amphetamine was available by prescription in tablet form and was used in the treatment of the sleeping disorder narcolepsy. The chemical structure of methamphetamine is similar to that of amphetamine, but it has more pronounced effects on the central nervous system. These drugs became known collectively as ATS, or amphetamine-type stimulants.

During World War II, ATS was widely used to keep the fighting men of the armies of several countries going. Both dextroamphetamine (Dexedrine) and methamphetamine (Methedrine) also became readily available. The German military was especially notorious for its use of methamphetamine, and it was rumored that Adolf Hitler himself received daily doses of a mixture that contained certain essential vitamins and amphetamines. Pilots in the German Luftwaffe were given chocolate dosed with methamphetamine, which became known in German as *Fliegerschokolade*, or "flyer's chocolate." Ordinary soldiers had to be content with the more common variety of methamphetamines, dispensed under the trade name Pervitin. But methamphetamine use was not confined to the German armed forces. Methamphetamines were also used by the US and Japanese armies fighting in rough and harsh conditions in Asia's warzones.

When the war was over, large quantities of amphetamines and meth-amphetamines, which the Japanese army had stockpiled for its troops, became available under the common street name *shabu*. It was banned in 1951, but the Japanese underworld, the *yakuza*, continued to produce it in clandestine laboratories. Stung by crackdowns in Japan, the smelly labora-tories were moved to South Korea and Taiwan, and later to the Philippines and mainland China. The demand was high in Japan, as the country was being rebuilt after the war. Construction workers, long-distance truck drivers, and other laborers were the main consumers. In more recent years younger people have become addicted to *shabu* and it is still a major social problem in Japan, even if trendier youngsters prefer more "up-market" drugs such as cocaine and ecstasy. *Shabu* has also established significant markets in the Philippines and Taiwan.

According to Andrew Weil, an American doctor who has written extensively about mind-altering drugs, for many years after ATS had been invented they were actually tolerated and their use was even encouraged by authorities. Weil mentions that governments of several countries, among them the Soviet Union, experimented with giving ATS to factory workers, "hoping to make them more productive (which, in the long run, they failed to do)." Doctors in the United States have prescribed ATS "for even more questionable reasons," according to Weil: "In the 1950s and 1960s, the US pharmaceutical industry manufactured enormous quan-tities of amphetamines (many of which turned up on the black market). The companies urged doctors to prescribe their products for depressed housewives and people with weight problems."

In Thailand, "speed" drugs were first marketed as an over-the-coun-ter stimulant that was brought to Thailand in 1955 by a South Korean company and became very popular. At the time, the tablets had a horse's head and the word "London" on them. They became known as *yama*, or horse drug, and, because of their brain-stimulating qualities, were used to treat patients suffering from narcolepsy and obesity. But the drug was subsequently withdrawn from pharmacies and hospitals when serious side effects were discovered.

However, *yama* found a new place outside of the medical service as a recreational drug. Researchers divide the history of ATS abuse in Thailand into three periods. The first, from the late 1950s to 1979, is called the amphetamine period, with abuse largely confined to long-distance truck and bus drivers, unskilled laborers, and students studying for examinations. Although limited to certain sectors of society, abuse became prevalent throughout the country and a serious problem. In 1967, to cope with the situation, the Thai government took various actions such as designating amphetamine as "narcotics in the same schedule as heroin." By criminalizing ATS, it became more dangerous to buy and sell it, and abuse rapidly decreased in the 1970s. By 1979 the authorities seemed to have the situation under control.

Then followed the so-called look-alike amphetamines period from 1980 to 1990. These drugs were bogus amphetamines containing varying amounts of caffeine, ephedrine, pseudoephedrine, and phenylpropanomine. These were sold as speed and purported to be authentic amphetamines. They did have a certain effect, but not nearly as great as that of real amphetamine. New legislation was introduced to control the sale of raw materials for these look-alike amphetamines, and they vanished from the scene in 1990. Real *yama* was also available during this period, but not to the same extent as in the 1970s.

After the bogus amphetamines came the third period: the methamphetamine period. This was a new stimulant that actually had been synthesized in laboratories in Bangkok and upcountry since 1988. But in the beginning the laboratories were small and operated on an irregular basis. Operators would often produce a batch of finished product, disassemble the makeshift laboratory, and either store it or move in to a different location while they acquired additional chemicals.

In 1990, as methamphetamine addiction began to spread across the country, the laboratories became more permanent—and the Thai police began to raid them. Laboratories were found and destroyed in several provinces in the central plains, among them Singburi, Ang Thong, and Suphanburi. In the same year, the Thai Public Health Ministry estimated that about half the country's 230,000 truck drivers used methamphetamines. In 1993 more than 70,000 students were identified as users.

Other estimates were even higher. A survey conducted in 1991 by doctors at Bangkok's Ramathibodi Hospital revealed the startling fact that 100 percent of truck drivers from northern Thailand used meth-amphetamines regularly. The figure for drivers from the northeast was 84.6 percent, and in the central plains 57.1 percent. The pills were also becoming killers. In early 1990 a ten-wheeled truck came hurtling across the crowded Sathorn Bridge in Bangkok and piled into the back of several vehicles waiting at the traffic lights. Four people died in the carnage, including a young police officer and a high-ranking Interior Ministry official. The accident was blamed on brake failure but, as usually happens in Thailand, the driver fled the scene. It was widely suspected that he was high on methamphetamine.

When *yama* became known as *yaba* the vast majority of users were no longer truck drivers, but youngsters aged fourteen to twenty-five—and there were many more varieties of the drug. In 1997 the ONCB listed ninety available types of *yaba* pills. The most common were an orange-red pill, but white, green, and blue versions (depending on what laboratory they had come from) were also on the list. More varieties have since been added to the list, but the most powerful and widely known pill has the letters "WY" imprinted on it. The green ones are also popular and have nicknames such as *khiaw morakot* ("emerald green"), *khiaw pak thung* ("dustbin-liner green"), *maa morakot* ("emerald horse"), and *marutayu see khiaw* ("satanic green").

Most are suitable for heating and inhaling, while other pills with more repulsive tastes are swallowed with liquid. Inhaling has an instant effect on the user. It is also possible to crush the pills and inject them intravenously, in which case the effect is again immediate. But that is not common. One of the reasons why methamphetamines have gained such a wide market is because using those kinds of drugs is not attached to the same social stigma as injecting heroin, while still delivering an instant high.

If the pills were swallowed, it would take about twenty minutes for the user to become intoxicated, so that method is not very common. Like the German *Fliegerschokolade*, some pills for sale in Thailand are laced with chocolate to make them more appealing to youngsters.

Yaba is taken by young people before going to discotheques, during motorcycle races, and when watching football matches. It is also popular among young males as it increases their sexual appetite and prowess.

And young Thais, regardless of who they are, usually take the drug in groups. According to French researcher Joël Meissonnier: "Often amphetamine-type stimulants are used in combination with other permitted stimulants, particularly spirits and beer. But whatever the combination of drugs and activities, the single common denominator is that all permutations involve group activities. *Yaba* can therefore be termed as a premier social drug."

Yaba is also taken by less fortunate groups in Thailand: migrant workers and refugees from Burma. In Chiang Mai, in the north, most construction workers in the 1990s were ethnic Shans from Burma who were working in the country illegally—and given *yaba* to work even harder. At the border town of Mae Sot, in the 1990s, there were seventy companies that employed overworked and underpaid Burmese laborers. Many of those workers became addicted to *yaba*, as did some 70 percent of the prostitutes in Mae Sot, most of whom had come from across the border. In Ranong in southern Thailand the local fishing industry employed at least ten thousand Burmese until the devastating tsunami of December 2004 gushed forth from the Andaman Sea. According to local sources, the Thai ship owners forced their Burmese crews to take a *yaba* pill every morning before they left port. It was meant to enhance the men's capacity to work, but many became addicted and began to spend their hard-earned money on drugs. At least one thousand Burmese fishermen died in the tsunami—no one knows the exact figure because they were working illegally in Thailand and therefore never registered with the authorities—and many went home after the disaster, as a large number of fishing boats were destroyed by the wave. But some remain, and others have come since the Thai fishing industry has begun to recover. The *yaba* dealers are back as well, selling drugs to whoever wants to buy—including impoverished migrant workers from Burma.

Yaba can also be a killer drug, sometimes in extremely tragic circumstances. In February 1999, Supatra Chompoosri, a forty-eight-year-old housewife, confessed to police in Chiang Rai that she had hired a gunman to kill her twenty-seven-year-old son, Sithipol Netsuwan. He had been his mother's darling until *yaba* made him a monster. Supatra said she could not bear the pain of witnessing her son hurting society and himself by selling and using *yaba*. He had been a police sergeant at Mae Chan in Chiang Rai but was discharged when he was implicated in stealing eighty thousand methamphetamine tablets seized from a trafficker. His addiction changed him from a decent man to "a person with a quick temper who could be harmful even to his own family," Supatra told the *Bangkok Post* of February 4, 1999. So she had him killed, "out of love and my concern for society," Supatra said. She was arrested along with the gunman she had paid forty-five thousand baht (about US$1,500) to put a bullet in her son's head.

THE END TO THE TRAGIC DRUG PRODUCTION IN THE GOLDEN TRIANGLE?

During a visit in February 2006 to Doi Tung, a mountain in northern Thailand where a program for the eradication of opium poppies has been carried out successfully over the years, Dr. Antonio Maria Costa, executive director of the United Nations Office on Drugs and Crime (UNODC), proudly stated: "We are indeed reaching a closure of the very tragic chapter of poppy cultivation in this part of the world." He also predicted that Thailand's neighbor Burma—still a major opium producer—would be added to the UN's list of opium-free nations in the near future.

His prediction was way off target. While Thailand has eradicated commercial opium production on its side of the border, poppies still bloom in the mountains of Burma every cold season. Production in Burma may have decreased in recent years, but the country is far from becoming opium-free. And, more importantly, the narcotics barons are shifting from producing heroin to making *yaba* and other types of ATS—but combating those kinds of drugs does not fall within the UNODC's limited mandate, so it is left out of the agency's annual drug surveys.

The UNODC does train customs and law enforcement agencies in Southeast Asia. But this is usually done at regional conferences where no one mentions a fundamental hurdle that must be overcome if any drug eradication program is to be successful: official complicity in the trade. Without the support and protection of powerful and influential individuals it would never be possible to trade the huge quantities of drugs that is the case in Southeast Asia today. Although some police forces in the region may be corrupt, others are actually effective—but their hands are often tied because they cannot move against persons who enjoy high-level protection. Narcotics intelligence officers can often do little more than collect and compile information about drug traffickers, their accomplices, and the companies with which they are associated. It is the small-time dealers who get whacked, as the 2003 "war on drugs" clearly demonstrated.

Proceeds from the drug trade are invested in legitimate enterprises such as nightclubs, karaoke parlors, hotels, petrol stations, construction companies, and even fruit farms. Black money is laundered white, playing an important role in the local economies of countries that produce or consume narcotics. The legitimate activities of the drug lords, built on proceeds gained from skyrocketing addiction rates, are in turn also profitable. But these were initially made possible only because of profits from the drug trade. Hong Kong researcher Yiu Kong Chu once concluded that the Triads (Chinese organized crime gangs active in the territory) "are indeed an integral rather than a mere predatory element of many sectors of the economy." The same could be said of Southeast Asia's drug lords and their respective countries.

Drug money also buys power and influence, as does income from other illegal activities such as prostitution, diesel oil smuggling, trafficking labor, gambling, illegal logging, and trading in contraband arms. Unauthorized gambling may be the biggest informal money-spinner in Thailand, but the drug trade is also extremely important and profitable.

In its 1997 survey, the Thai Public Health Ministry estimated that, based on the assumption that a million addicts and occasional users consumed on average two pills daily, the money being spent on *yaba* was 190 million baht a day, or 69.35 billion baht a year. Using the exchange rate at the time, that is US$7.6 million a day and US$2.774 billion per year. The trade may not give the young street pushers in Chiang Mai much to rejoice over, as they have to supplement their meager incomes by selling sexual services. But others have become immensely rich as a result.

The drug trade, furthermore, involves many more actors on different levels than other illegal activities. In criticizing official US narcotics policies, researchers Alfred W. McCoy and Alan A. Block have argued that "treating global narcotics trafficking as if it were a localized vice such as pornography or prostitution, US drug agencies often apply repression without any awareness of the intricate dynamics of these global marketing systems." The local approach to the drug problem in Southeast Asia from a law enforcement perspective is not very different from that of the United States. But it is not possible to fight the drug trade without analyzing underlying political and—in Southeast Asia—ethnic factors. The trade in *yaba* may not be global in the same way as the heroin business, but, as the syndicates and the networks that used to deal in heroin are often identical with those now producing and marketing *yaba*, the fundamental political, historical, and social roots of the problem remain the same.

This could be seen quite clearly when, following several crackdowns in Thailand in the early 1990s, production moved across the border to Burma. The shift was made possible by some tumultuous events in the remote northeastern mountains of that country in the spring of 1989.

FIGURE 2. Map of Shan State

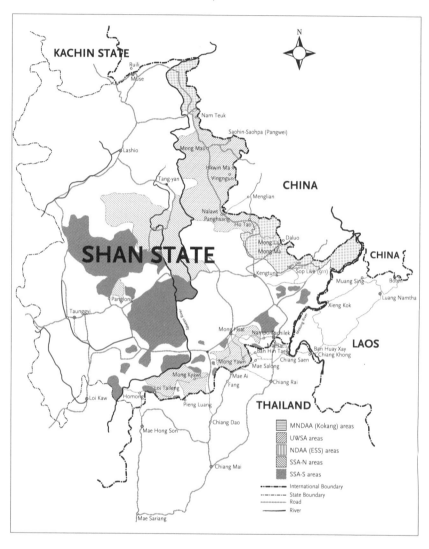

MNDAA (Kokang) areas
UWSA areas
NDAA (ESS) areas
SSA-N areas
SSA-S areas
International Boundary
State Boundary
Road
River

TWO

THE MUTINY

ONE OF Asia's longest communist insurrections ended on the night of April 16, 1989. Its cessation was not the outcome of a successful government offensive or generous amnesty policy but of an all-out mutiny within the rank and file of the Communist Party of Burma (CPB). That night, thousands of mutineers stormed the CPB's headquarters at Panghsang, a small town near the Chinese frontier in the Wa Hills of Burma's northeastern Shan State. The rebellious troops seized the well-stocked armory and other buildings. While they were smashing portraits of communist icons Marx, Engels, Lenin, Stalin, and Mao Zedong, and destroying CPB literature in an outburst of anti-party feeling, the CPB's aging, staunchly Maoist leadership fled across the Nam Hka border river to China. For the first time in history, a communist insurgency had been defeated by a movement within its own ranks.

The tumultuous event at Panghsang on April 16–17 came after years of simmering discontent with the old leadership, which had stubbornly refused to give up an increasingly anachronistic political line unchanged since the days of the Cultural Revolution in China in the late 1960s. Even more importantly, the mutiny reflected ethnic tensions within the party. The overwhelming majority of the CPB's troops came from various minority peoples in the rugged and remote Sino-Burmese border mountains, and these individuals have always been motivated by ethnic and generally anti-government sentiments rather than ideology. An estimated 80 percent of the rank and file of the army were Wa, a tribal people from the Sino-Burmese border mountains who had been headhunters before the CPB, with Chinese assistance, gained control over the area in the late 1960s and early 1970s. Nearly all of the CPB's military commanders were also from various ethnic groups—some Wa, but mostly Kokang Chinese, Kachin, Shan, and others—with aging Burman Marxist-Leninists only as party leaders and as political commissars attached to the various units.

Another important factor behind the mutiny was the lucrative drug trade in the CPB's base area. During the CPB's third—and last—party congress, held in 1985, it was decided to take stern measures against opium trading, the manufacture of its derivative heroin, and other "illegal activities" in which local commanders had become involved. For decades opium had been the main cash crop in the CPB's area and the party had levied a 10 percent tax on growers and traders. But the importance of the opium trade increased as power patterns changed in the region, in particular the new foreign policy adopted by China after the death of Mao Zedong in 1976.

The CPB had received massive support from China in the 1960s and 1970s—as had other communist parties in the region—but with Beijing's drive to modernize its economy and promote foreign trade, aid to those parties was drastically reduced. The cutback in Chinese aid led to the almost immediate collapse of the Communist Party of Thailand (CPT) and the final demise of the Communist Party of Malaya (CPM). In Burma, however, the communist insurrection continued—although the reduction in Chinese aid severely affected the CPB's ability to equip its troops and to maintain schools and hospitals in the territory under its control. This forced the CPB to introduce heavy and unpopular taxes—not only on opium—on the population in its "liberated area," further alienating the leadership from the local people in the northeastern border mountains.

At the same time, local commanders had begun to act more independently of Panghsang—and discovered that there were significant profits to be made from the local opium trade. Party agents were sent to check up on them and report any "wrongdoing" to the center. More specifically, the CPB leadership announced that any party member found to be involved in the opium trade, other than just taxing it, would face "severe punishment." Anyone caught with two kilograms or more of heroin—which now was being produced by local commanders in the CPB's base area—would face execution.

The involvement of CPB cadres in the drug trade had become an embarrassment to the party's ideologically motivated leadership. It is also plausible to assume that the campaign had been launched under Chinese pressure. The spillover of drugs from the CPB's base area into China was becoming a problem, and increasing amounts of heroin were also being smuggled to Hong Kong via Kunming, the capital of Yunnan province, which borders Burma.

One of the authors of this book wrote in the June 4, 1987, issue of the Hong Kong weekly *Far Eastern Economic Review*: "If strictly enforced, the policy could create serious conflicts between the CPB's ideologically motivated top leadership and the party's many local cadres who are benefiting from the drug trade. This puts the whole feasibility of the [anti-drug] campaign into question, and most local observers believe it likely that the campaign will eventually be abandoned to prevent a split in the party." The campaign was never abandoned and the inevitable happened.

Already, in 1981, the Chinese had actually begun offering asylum to CPB leaders and high-ranking cadres. This offer included a modest government pension (250 renminbi, or US$36, a month for a Politburo member; 200 renminbi, or US$29, for a member of the Central Committee; 180 renminbi, or US$26, for any other leading cadre; and 100 renminbi, or US$15, for ordinary party members), a house, and a plot of land, on condition that the retired CPB cadres refrained from political activity of any kind in China. The old guard, who had lived in China during the Cultural Revolution and been close to Mao Zedong, saw the offer as treachery, although they never criticized China openly. The offer was repeated in 1985 and again in 1988. Some of the younger, lower-ranking CPB cadres accepted the offer, but none of the top leaders.

In early 1989 the Chinese once again approached the CPB and tried to persuade the leadership to give up and retire in China so that the border with Burma could be opened to bilateral trade between the two countries. A crisis meeting was convened on February 20 at Panghsang. For the first time, the CPB chairman, the seventy-five-year-old Thakin Ba Thein Tin, lashed out against the Chinese. In an address to the secret meeting, he referred to "misunderstandings in our relations with a sister party. Even if there are differences between us, we have to coexist and adhere to the principle of noninterference in each other's affairs. This is the same as in 1981, 1985, and 1988. *We* have no desire to become revisionists."

The minutes of that secret meeting were leaked, and this may have encouraged the disgruntled rank and file to rise up against the old leadership. A major reason why the mutiny did not happen earlier was that the soldiers and local commanders were uncertain of China's reaction to such a move. After all, the CPB leaders still went to China every now and then—and they were always picked up at the border by Chinese officials in limousines; the complexities of regional politics were beyond the comprehension of most CPB cadres and soldiers.

On March 12, units in Kokang—part of Burma, and the CPB's base area, but populated by ethnic Chinese—took the first step and openly challenged the CPB leadership. Led by Peng Jiasheng, a local CPB commander already heavily involved in the opium trade, they broke away from the party and also captured Möng Ko, an important CPB base and border town west of the Salween river. The mutiny quickly spread to all other CPB base areas along the Chinese frontier. When Panghsang fell, the mutineers also took over the party's old radio station. On April 18 they broadcast the first denouncement of what they termed "the narrow racial policies of the Communist Party of Burma." An even stronger broadcast followed on April 28:

> Conditions were good before 1979. But what has the situation come to now? No progress whatsoever is being made. Why? In our opinion, it is because some leaders are clinging to power and are obstinately pursuing an erroneous line. They are divorced from reality, practicing individualism and sectarianism, failing to study and analyze local and foreign conditions, and ignoring actual material conditions . . . They have cheated the people of the Wa region, and through lies and propaganda have dragged us into their sham revolution . . . How can an enemy with modern weapons be defeated by an empty ideology and through military methods that do not integrate theory with practice? We, the people of the Wa region, never kowtow before an aggressor army whether it be local or foreign. Although we are poor and backward in terms of culture and literature, we are very strong in our determination. What became of the lives of people of the Wa region following the wresting of power by an evil-minded individual within the CPB at a certain time in the past? It was a hard life for the people. The burden on the people became heavier with more taxes being levied. We faced grave hardships. Can the people avoid staging an uprising under such a condition?

It is uncertain who that "evil-minded individual" was. But within a month of the initial uprising in Kokang the CPB had ceased to exist—almost fifty years after it had been founded by a group of young Burmese intellectuals in a small apartment on Barr Street around the corner from Rangoon's colonial-style City Hall, and forty-one years since it decided to resort to armed struggle against the government, which it did a year after Burma's independence in 1948. Burma's aging communists and their families—about three hundred people—ended up in exile in China. The leaders retired in Kunming, where most of them died in the late 1990s and early 2000s. Some of the younger cadres became small traders in Tengchong, Ruili, and towns along the Sino-Burmese border.

THE RISE AND FALL OF BURMA'S COMMUNIST MOVEMENT

China had shown only scant interest in Burma's communist rebellion as long as the country was ruled by the democratically elected government of Prime Minister U Nu. In the early 1950s a handful of party leaders, among them Thakin Ba Thein Tin, had trekked to China, where they were allowed to stay in a settlement near Chengdu, in Sichuan province. Then a new era in Burmese insurgency was ushered in after the chief of the Burmese army, General Ne Win, seized power in a coup d'état in 1962. Ethnic rebellions, which had plagued Burma since independence, flared anew—and for the first time the CPB began receiving open support from China. Pamphlets denouncing Ne Win's new military regime were printed in Beijing, and in late 1963 CPB cadres began surveying possible infiltration routes from Yunnan into northeastern Burma. China built a network of asphalt highways leading from Kunming to various points along the borders with Burma and Laos, where another communist movement was active.

The plan was to build up a new CPB base area adjacent to the Chinese frontier, and from there push down to central Burma, where smaller and badly equipped units of communist guerrilla forces were still holding out in the Pegu Yoma mountains, north of Rangoon, and other pockets elsewhere in the country. In 1967, anti-Chinese riots in Rangoon—orchestrated by Burma's military authorities to deflect public anger at a rapidly deteriorating economy—provided a convenient excuse for the Chinese to intervene directly in Burma's civil war.

On New Year's Day, 1968, the first armed CPB units entered northeastern Burma from Yunnan. They never managed to reach the old units in the Pegu Yoma, but they built up a 20,000 sq. km. base area along the Chinese frontier and an army of nearly twenty thousand men. During the decade 1968–78, China poured more aid into the CPB effort than any other communist movement outside Indochina. Assault rifles, machineguns, rocket launchers, anti-aircraft guns, radio equipment, jeeps, trucks, petrol, maps of the area, and even rice, cooking oil, other foodstuff, and kitchen utensils were sent across the frontier into the CPB's new revolutionary base area. The Chinese also built hydroelectric power stations inside the area, and the clandestine radio station, *People's Voice of Burma*, began transmitting from the Yunnan side of the frontier in April 1971, continuing to do so until the mutineers took it over in April 1989. Thousands of Chinese "volunteers" also streamed across the border to provide additional support to the CPB.

Since the population in the CPB's new northeastern base area was not Burman, but hilltribe, the communists enlisted the support of local warlords in the area. Among them were Chao Ngi Lai from the northern Wa Hills and Bao Youxiang from the wild, headhunting area around Hkwin Ma in the heart of rugged border mountains. The communists could provide their local private armies with modern weapons to fight their enemies, who were rival warlords. Ideology was not an important issue for commanders such as Chao and Bao, but without them the CPB would never have been able to conquer the Wa Hills. In the end, when the party became poorer and the Burman leaders older and more out of touch with reality, the warlords turned against them.

When the once-mighty party collapsed in 1989, it subsequently split up into four different, regional armies based along ethnic lines:

1. The Burma National United Party and Army, which was set up by the Wa component of the ex-CPB army. It was led by Chao and Bao. They had actually become alternate members of the CPB's Central Committee at the third party congress in 1985, the only Was in any prominent position

in the party hierarchy, but their loyalty to the old party had never been strong. They now contacted a group of non-communist Was along the Thai border, who had been driven south by the communists in the early 1970s. The two enemy forces merged and, in November 1989, became the United Wa State Party and Army (UWSP/UWSA). At the time of the merger it had more than fifteen thousand regular and irregular soldiers under its command. It was to grow even stronger during the 1990s.

2. The Myanmar National Democratic Alliance Army (MNDAA), led by the first mutineer, Peng Jiasheng, and his younger brother Peng Jiafu, became the new unit in Kokang—which traditionally produces the best opium in Southeast Asia. The initial strength of the MNDAA was approximately 1,500 to 2,000 men.

3. The National Democratic Alliance Army (Eastern Shan State)—sometimes referred to as the Shan State Army (East) or the 369 area—in the hills north of Kengtung where the borders of Burma, China, and Laos meet, was the name of the third ex-CPB grouping. It was led by Lin Mingxian and Zhang Zhiming, who were among the few former Red Guards from Yunnan who had joined the CPB during the Cultural Revolution and stayed on when China recalled most of the volunteers. The area under their control around the town of Möng La was also very rich in opium, but sparsely populated. The strength of their army at the time of the mutiny was estimated at 3,500 to 4,000 men. Lin Mingxian had married the daughter of Kokang drug lord Peng Jiasheng, and their groups developed close ties.

4. The New Democratic Army (NDA), with fewer than one thousand men, is the smallest of the former CPB forces. Since the mutiny, it has been led by Ting Ying and Zalum and its area of operation is around the Kambaiti, Pangwa, and Hpimaw passes on the Yunnan frontier in Kachin State. Although some poppies have always been grown near Kambaiti, this was never a major drug producing area.

Suddenly, there was no longer any communist insurgency in Burma, only ethnic rebel armies. The breakup of the CPB also came at a time when central Burma was in turmoil. In August and September 1988, millions of people from virtually every town and major village across the country had taken to the streets to demand an end to twenty-six years of stifling military rule and the restoration of democracy that existed before the 1962 coup d'état. The protests shook Burma's military establishment, which responded fiercely. Thousands of people were gunned down as the army moved in to shore up a regime overwhelmed by popular protests. The crushing of the 1988 uprising was more dramatic and much bloodier than the better publicized events in Beijing's Tiananmen Square a year later.

In the wake of the massacres in Rangoon and elsewhere in the country, more than eight thousand pro-democracy activists fled the urban centers for the border areas near Thailand, where a multitude of ethnic insurgencies, not involved in the drug trade, were active. Significantly, the main drug-funded force operating along the border, Khun Sa and his Möng Tai Army (MTA), refused to shelter any dissidents who had fled the urban areas; his main interest was business, not fighting the government.

The Burmese military now feared a renewed, potentially dangerous insurgency along its frontiers: a possible alliance between the ethnic rebels and the pro-democracy activists from Rangoon and other towns and cities. But these Thai border-based groups—Karen, Mon, Karenni, and Pa-O— were unable to provide the urban dissidents with more than a handful of weapons. In 1988 none of the ethnic armies could match the strength of the CPB, with its then still-strong army and relatively large base area along the Sino-Burmese border in the northeast. Unlike the ethnic insurgents, the CPB also had vast quantities of arms and ammunition. The communists were not as strong as before, but they had a substantial arsenal that was left over from the aid that China had provided in the 1960s and 1970s. It was enough for at least ten years of guerrilla warfare against the central government in Rangoon.

Despite government claims of a "communist conspiracy" behind the 1988 uprising, there was at that time no link between the anti-totalitarian, pro-democracy movement in central Burma and the orthodox, Marxist-Leninist leadership of the CPB. However, given the strong desire for revenge for the bloody events of 1988, it is plausible to assume that urban dissidents would have accepted arms from any source. Thus it became imperative for the new junta that had seized power on September 18, 1988—the State

Law and Order Restoration Council (SLORC)—to neutralize as many of the border insurgencies as possible, especially the CPB. With the 1989 mutiny the situation became even more precarious for Burma's military government, as an alliance between the "old" ethnic armies, the urban dissidents, and the "new" ones, which emerged after the collapse of the CPB, could now become reality.

Soon after the breakup of the old party, the ethnic rebels sent a delegation from the Thai border to Panghsang to negotiate with the CPB mutineers, but the authorities in Rangoon reacted faster, with more determination—and with much more to offer than the ethnic rebels. Within weeks of the CPB mutiny, the then powerful chief of Burma's military intelligence, Major General Khin Nyunt, took a helicopter up to the border area to meet personally with Peng Jiafu, Chao Ngi Lai, and other leaders of the mutiny.

Step by step, alliances of convenience were forged between Burma's military authorities and various groups of mutineers. In exchange for promises not to attack government forces and to sever ties with other rebel groups, the CPB mutineers were granted unofficial permission to engage in any kind of business to sustain themselves—which in Burma's remote and underdeveloped hill areas inevitably meant opium production. Rangoon also promised to launch a "border-development program" in the former CPB areas, and the United Nations and its various agencies were invited to help fund those projects.

The success in striking those deals with the ex-CPB forces was largely due to the efforts of Lo Hsing-han, a Kokang Chinese ex-warlord who acted as an intermediary with the mutineers. In the early 1970s he had been dubbed the "King of the Golden Triangle" and the "King of Heroin," and led a government-recognized militia unit under a program called Ka Kwe Ye (KKY). The program had been initiated in 1963, at a time when Rangoon was incapable of overcoming the country's innumerable rebel armies. In exchange for fighting the rebels, the various KKY forces were given the right to use all government-controlled roads and towns in Shan State for opium smuggling. By allowing them to trade in opium, the Burmese government hoped that the KKY militias would be self-supporting; there was hardly any money in the central coffers in Rangoon to support a sustained counterinsurgency campaign at this stage.

Many KKY commanders actually became rich on the deal. The most famous were Lo, the chief of Kokang KKY, and Zhang Qifu, alias Khun Sa, who headed the KKY unit in Loi Maw near the Burmese army's garrison town of Tang-yan. Lo had fought alongside the Burmese army against the CPB in the early 1970s, and Khun Sa guarded the western banks of the Salween river, opposite CPB strongholds in the Wa Hills.

But the KKY program became a failure as the local militia commanders had to negotiate tax agreements with the rebels, who controlled the countryside through which they had to conduct their drug convoys down to the Thai border, where the opium was sold to private merchants. Thus, in 1972, the KKY units were ordered to disband. Lo, however, refused to do so. He went underground and teamed up with the Shan State Army (SSA), at that time the most powerful ethnic rebel army in Shan State. But he was captured in August 1973 when he slipped across the border into Thailand to escape a Burmese army attack.

Lo was extradited to Burma, where he was sentenced to death, not for trading in opium—for that he had Rangoon's unofficial permission—but for "rebellion against the state," a reference to his brief alliance with the SSA. But Rangoon was farsighted enough not to execute Lo; that would have been tantamount to destroying a useful political tool. He was released during a general amnesty in 1980 and given two million kyats in Burmese currency to build a new military camp at the so-called Salween Village in the Nampawng area southwest of Lashio. Moreover, he set up a *pyi thu sit*, or "people's militia" unit, which was modeled after the infamous KKY home guards of the 1960s and early 1970s. The new *pyi thu sit* units were not as powerful as the old KKY, but the agreement between them and the central authorities was basically the same—and between Burma's military rulers and the former CPB forces.

It was several years before Lo regained his former strength and prominence, however. The 1989 mutiny within the CPB came at the right time, and on March 20–21, 1989, only a week after the first uprising in Kokang, he paid his first visit to his native Kokang area, which had been under CPB control since 1968. This visit paved the way for Khin Nyunt's first meetings with the mutineers—and the remarkable cease-fire agreements, which were struck between Burma's military government and thousands of former insurgents. Another intermediary who helped initiate contacts between the CPB mutineers in Kokang and the government in Rangoon was Olive Yang, an old "warlady" and a native of Kokang, who had been instrumental in building up the Golden Triangle opium trade in the late 1950s and early 1960s.

The CPB mutiny also provided Lo with a golden opportunity to rebuild his former drug empire. Apart from being a local home guard commander, Lo had until the mutiny been little more than a small-scale entrepreneur, running bus companies, video parlors, and liquor franchises. Since the CPB mutiny, and the role he played as a mediator between the government and the former CPB forces, he and his son Steven Law have grown to become two of Burma's most prominent businessmen and their multifaceted conglomerate, Asia World, has interests in the hotel industry, transport, road construction, timber, gems, and the import and export of various legal commodities. The evidence may be circumstantial, but it is beyond doubt that the initial capital for their legitimate businesses must have come from the drug trade; there is simply no other possible source, and the timing of their rise from obscurity to prominence seems far more than a coincidence.

BURMA'S NEW GROWTH INDUSTRY

In the late 1980s, Burma's opium production suddenly more than doubled as a result of the cease-fire agreements with the former CPB forces. According to the United States government, the 1987 harvest for Burma yielded 836 tons of raw opium; by 1995, production had increased to 2,340 tons. Satellite imagery showed that the area under poppy cultivation increased from 92,300 hectares in 1987 to 142,700 in 1989 and 154,000 in 1995. By the mid 1990s, Burma's opium production reached 2,000 tons, up from 350–600 tons annually before the CPB mutiny. Furthermore, the cease-fire agreements with the government also enabled the former CPB forces to bring in chemicals, mainly acetic anhydrite—which is needed to convert raw opium into heroin—by truck from India. Within a few years after the mutiny, intelligence sources were able to locate at least seventeen new heroin refineries in Kokang and adjacent areas, six in the Wa Hills and two in Lin Mingxian's area north of Kengtung, where the town of Möng La opposite Daluo in Yunnan developed into one of the most important drug-running centers in the country.

The heroin trade took off with a speed that caught almost every observer of the Southeast Asia drug scene by surprise. It takes ten kilograms of raw opium to make one kilogram of heroin, and after deducting the amount of opium that is usually smoked locally, Burma's potential heroin output soared from 54 tons in 1987 to 166 tons in 1995, making drugs the impoverished and mismanaged country's only growth industry. In Möng La—the first real boom town in the former CPB's area—the proceeds from the trade were invested in casinos, hotels, bars, and, incredibly, a "drug eradication museum." Officially, Lin Mingxian was in charge of an anti-drug campaign in his area, and began to receive delegations from various United Nations agencies, including personnel in charge of its drug control program. Post-mutiny Möng La also received thousands of tourists daily from China, who came across the border in chartered tour buses. Main attractions included a lavish transvestite show imported from Thailand, and, for a while, a group of prostitutes from Russia and the Ukraine.

Before long, Panghsang was also transformed into a bustling town of some twenty-five thousand residents, with modern buildings and paved roads. During the days of the CPB, its only concrete houses were a cluster of buildings where the party leaders resided, and the broadcasting station where important meetings were also held. The rest consisted of huts made of wood and bamboo, and the only commercial activity was an old-fashioned marketplace where locals sold vegetables, pork, chickens—and opium, which was readily available and taxed by the party. Occasionally, traders from China came across to sell clothes, toys, and trinkets, or ice cream from boxes they carried on the backs of bicycles.

On a hill overlooking Panghsang, adjacent to what used to a memorial to fallen CPB comrades, now stands the Golden Baby Disco, a two-storey structure. The upper level is a nightclub with a glass wall offering a view of the lights of Panghsang by night. The lower level has karaoke lounges with private party rooms where VIPs can entertain their guests—and, for an extra fee, buy the company of young hostesses in skimpy miniskirts. Not far from the Golden Baby Disco is a large casino operated by the UWSA's Ying Yuang Entertainment Corporation. Across the street is a wooded rest area where several moon bears and a monkey are kept in cages. They are given beer and lit cigarettes by onlookers, and look quite miserable.

Commercial sex is available not only in the karaoke lounges. Panghsang's many hair salons double as venues to employ prostitutes at night under pink neon lights. For a fee the women can be taken to nearby hotels. No doubt Thakin Ba Thein Tin and his old CPB comrades would turn in their graves if they could see what had become of their headquarters, from where they tried to launch a proletarian revolution in Burma.

Today, Panghsang even has its own bank, the Wa Pang, or Wa State, Bank, which is located on the main road. Cars parked outside include luxury sedans and SUVs with number plates issued by the local Wa authorities. There is a cinema, a day market, a bumper car arena, and a roller skating rink where skates can be rented by the hour. One of the UWSA commanders even had a bowling alley built for him and his close associates. It was open to the public but with a private lane reserved for the Wa leaders. Neatly uniformed UWSA troops in formation can be seen drilling in town as Wa police vehicles patrol the streets. Signs tell visitors not to step over the flowerbeds that separate the lanes of the main roads in Panghsang. Offenders are charged a hefty fine of 300 renminbi, or US$44.

Under the cease-fire agreement with the government, the Burmese military maintains a liaison office in Panghsang, staffed by about ten officers. But they rarely leave the compound in which they stay, and the only Burmese flag in Panghsang flies over a government-run clinic. All other official buildings fly the UWSA flag alongside the Wa State flag—a blue and red banner with a star, a sun, and a crossed dagger and spear. "The Wa Sate" has by all intents and purposes become a semi-independent, but unrecognized, buffer state between Burma and China, with its own laws and its own administration.

The new prosperity of places such as Panghsang and Möng La also shows quite clearly that profits from the drug trade have been enormous. One factor was that the string of new heroin refineries was conveniently located near the main growing areas in northern Burma, cutting out several middlemen. Equally important, they were close to the rapidly growing Chinese drug market and routes to the outside world through Yunnan that seemed easier than the old ways down to the Thai border, where heroin laboratories had been operating since the early 1970s. In the early 1990s, for the first time, the same laboratories in northern Burma also began to produce methamphetamines.

Ironically, at a time when almost the entire population of Burma had turned against the regime, thousands of former insurgents rallied behind the ruling military, lured by lucrative business opportunities and unofficial permission to trade in drugs with impunity.

With the collapse of the communist insurgency in 1989, several smaller ethnic armies also gave in. The two-thousand-strong SSA, which for decades had waged a war for autonomy for Shan State, made peace with Rangoon on September 24, 1989, and was granted timber concessions in the Hsipaw area in northern Shan State. They were followed by smaller groups of Pa-O and Palaung rebels who also operated in Shan State.

The Kachin Independence Army (KIA), which with eight thousand men in arms was Burma's most powerful ethnic rebel army, and which controlled most of Kachin State in the far north of the country, entered into an agreement with the SLORC in October 1993 and signed a formal cease-fire deal with Rangoon in February the following year. As a result, several pro-democracy activists who had fled to the KIA-controlled area surrendered in July 1994 and returned to the towns from which they had fled after the 1988 uprising. By 1997 more than a dozen ethnic rebel armies had made peace with Rangoon.

The threat from the border areas was thwarted, the regime was safe, but the consequences for the country, and the outside world, have been disastrous. Enormous quantities of heroin—and soon also methamphetamines—began to pour out of Burma in all directions, providing incomes for criminals far beyond the country's own borders.

CHINA: THE RETURN OF DRUG ABUSE

With the CPB out of the way, China and Burma could establish direct cross-border trade for the first time in decades. The first steps had already been taken when, on August 6, 1988, the two countries signed a bilateral border trade agreement. By then the days of Mao Zedong's support to communist movements in the region was well and truly over, and Deng Xiaoping's pragmatism was guiding Chinese foreign policy. This agreement was the first of its kind that hitherto isolated Burma had entered into with a neighbor. It was especially significant because it was signed at a time when Burma was in turmoil: two days later, the countrywide uprising broke out.

But the Chinese, renowned for their ability to plan far ahead, had expressed their intentions, almost unnoticed, in an article in the official weekly *Beijing Review* as early as September 2, 1985. Titled "Opening to the Southwest: An Expert Opinion," the article, written by the former vice-minister of communications, Pan Qi, outlined the possibilities of finding an outlet for trade from China's landlocked provinces of Yunnan, Sichuan, and Guizhou through Burma to the Indian Ocean. It mentioned the Burmese railheads of Myitkyina and Lashio in the north and northeast, and the Irrawaddy River as possible conduits for the export of goods from those provinces—but omitted to say that all relevant border areas, at that time, were not under Burmese central government control.

All that changed, of course, after the March–April 1989 mutiny. By late 1991, Chinese experts were assisting in a series of infrastructure projects to spruce up Burma's poorly maintained roads and railways. Border trade was booming—and China emerged as Burma's most important source of military hardware. Additional military equipment was provided by Pakistan, which has also helped Burma modernize its defense industries, by Singapore, and later even by North Korea. The total value of Chinese arms deliveries to Burma to date is not known, but intelligence sources estimate it to be about US$1.4 billion. Deliveries include fighter, ground attack, and transport aircraft, tanks and armored personnel carriers, naval vessels, a variety of towed and self-propelled artillery, surface-to-air missiles, trucks, and infantry equipment.

With the open border came heroin too. Before the 1949 communist takeover, China had vast poppy fields and millions of opium smokers, and addiction was considered the country's most serious social problem. The communists effectively put an end to both poppy cultivation and the sale of narcotics. The methods were brutal, but they worked. Scores of petty gangsters, opium dealers, and even addicts were rounded up and shot after summary trials. Other addicts were sent to rehabilitation centers—and the vast poppy fields in the Chinese interior were destroyed.

Then, in the early 1990s, drugs were back again—and this time mainly from the new refineries across the Burmese border. By the early 2000s, China had at least nine hundred thousand known drug addicts, and probably several million others who had not been registered by the authorities. Some unofficial estimates put the figure as high as twelve million. In 2001, 83.7 percent of the registered addicts were male and 73.9 percent were under the age of thirty-five.

The degree to which the influx of drugs and drug money had affected politics and society became clear in late 1992 when thousands of Chinese troops supported by tanks were forced to besiege a border town which had been taken over by drug traffickers.

The Chinese journal *People's Armed Police News* in its December 13, 1992, issue reported that a major military operation had been carried out against drug traffickers in southern China for "over two months beginning August 31." The target was Pingyuan, a town near the Vietnamese border, which served as a major smuggling center for Chinese contraband entering Vietnam before that border was also open to legal trade in late 1991.

The economy in the area was in the hands of ethnic Yunnanese Muslims—Panthays, or "Hui" as they are called in China, "Haw" in Thailand—who had dominated the caravan trade in the region for more than a century. Through their contacts throughout the Golden Triangle, and especially in the Hopang-Panglong area between Kokang and the Wa Hills, Panthay drug smuggling rings had built up an extensive network of routes from Burma through southern China, and on to regional and international markets.

By 1992 Pingyuan had become a "country within the country," giving safe haven to outlaws and bandits from across China, the unusual report in the *People's Armed Police News* stated. Thousands of heavily armed troops, supported by armor, eventually moved in.

When the eighty-day campaign was over, the Chinese commanders found luxury villas, bars, and dance halls run by the traffickers. Among them was Ma Siling (Ma, meaning "horse," is a common Panthay/Hui name), who was found living in a fortified villa in Pingyuan despite having been officially sentenced to death by a local court for drug trafficking.

Significantly, knowledge of the operation in Pingyuan was kept from the low-level officers in Yunnan. The net haul after the operation: 854 people arrested and 981 kilograms of drugs seized along with 353 assorted weapons. More than one thousand Chinese officers and privates received awards for "meritorious service in the operation," according to the *People's Armed Police News*.

Another drive against drug trafficking in Yunnan was launched in mid-1994. It followed the arrest on May 9 of Yang Muxian, a younger brother of Yang Muliang, a former CPB commander who after the mutiny had founded the Myanmar National Democratic Alliance Army (MNDAA) together with the Peng brothers. Yang Muxian was charged with smuggling hundreds of kilograms of heroin into Yunnan and he was executed in Kunming in October 1994 along with sixteen accomplices. Two of them were local police officers from the area and another two were police officers from the coastal province of Fujian. The involvement of the police reflected official complicity in the trade, while the presence of the Fujianese pointed at links with organized crime. The Chinese Triads, or secret societies, have always been strong among the Fujianese, who also dominate Chinatowns in Burma, Malaysia, and the USA.

Almost two hundred local border officials—including police, customs, and security personnel—were also detained in the wake of Yang's arrest, emphasizing the magnitude of official complicity in the trade, as well as widespread corruption in Yunnan. Again, the central authorities used the People's Armed Police to carry out the operation. The deployment of the PAP, the strike force of China's powerful internal security apparatus, to deal with the traffickers indicated that local authorities were unable, or even unwilling, to confront the growing drug problem in the country.

Officially, several of the former CPB commanders were barred from entering China because of their known involvement in the drug trade. But the fact that all of them had been operating for years along the Sino-Burmese border meant that they had long-standing working relationships with Chinese security authorities in Yunnan and perhaps even elsewhere.

A well-placed source from northeastern Burma insisted in an interview in early 1991 that this personal friendship enabled them to visit China regularly and own property across the border, including hotels and private houses. "Sometimes they are even escorted by Chinese security officials and driven around in their cars," the source alleged.

For reasons of border security, China did need to have at least a working relationship with the new and mighty UWSA, which controlled a long stretch of the common Sino-Burmese frontier. Somewhat paradoxically, the UWSA soon became stronger and better equipped than the CPB had ever been—and the new weaponry came from China. Nor have the Chinese severed ties with the KIA in the far north. China, obviously, is playing several games in Burma, and although it no longer seeks to export communist revolution, it wants to expand its economic influence down the Southeast Asian peninsula. And given the uncertain future of Burma's military regime, relations with a group like the UWSA secure a foothold for China inside the country.

A clear sign of Chinese approval of the UWSA presence across the border also came when, in November 2007, a new concrete bridge across the Nam Hka river was completed. It replaced the old, rickety steel and wooden bridge that had been there since the CPB days. The border crossing now resembles any similar crossing anywhere in Asia, and there is a steady traffic across the bridge with Chinese officials on one side and Wa on the other.

But the Wa leaders also had to deal with anger from the Chinese side. In 1995, UWSP leader Chao Ngi Lai suffered a stroke and was unable to carry out his duties, so UWSA commander Bao assumed the chairmanship of the party as well. Under his leadership the collection of raw opium and the production of heroin became more centralized.

Bao was summoned several times to Kunming and read the riot act: no drugs into China. The Chinese were growing increasingly frustrated as vast quantities of heroin were flowing across the border. In the early 1980s, heroin was almost unheard of in China, but in 1995 the authorities seized 2.376 tons of the drug. This jumped to 4.347 tons in 1996, 5.477 tons in 1997, 6.281 tons in 2000, and a record 13.2 tons in 2001. While smaller quantities of heroin enter China from the so-called Golden Crescent in Central

Asia—Afghanistan, Pakistan, and Tajikistan—nearly all of it comes from Burma. In 1991 there were 8,080 drug-related arrests in China. A decade later the number of arrests had increased to 40,854.

The number of those arrested who were then sentenced to death is not known, but China executes most prisoners convicted of serious drug offenses. When China celebrated the United Nations-declared Anti Drugs Day on June 26, 1996, it did so in its own way: by sentencing 769 drug offenders to death or life imprisonment. Many were taken immediately from the court room to the execution ground to be shot, and most executions were carried out in Kunming.

The answer from the Wa leadership was to switch to the production of drugs other than opium and its derivative, heroin—so they turned to methamphetamines, a synthetic drug that does not require laborious cultivation of any unpredictable crop that risks being destroyed by bad weather.

Synthetic drugs do have a market in China as well—but there they are locally produced in the country and therefore considered an internal problem. The market for methamphetamines produced in areas controlled by the UWSA and other former CPB forces is in Thailand, and increasingly also in Laos and Cambodia. Old networks were revitalized and old drug routes, which were almost severed when the main area in which heroin was refined shifted to the Chinese frontier, were once again open for traffic. Now it was time for a new drug, *yaba*, the scourge that is tearing Thai society apart.

FIGURE 3. Drug pusher arrested in Chiang Rai, northern Thailand, with *yaba*.

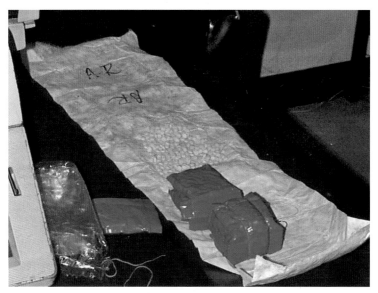

FIGURE 4. *Yaba* pills.

FIGURE 5 (ABOVE LEFT). Internal rotary mechanism of a nineteen-pill-per-cycle *yaba* pill compressor seized by Thai authorities in the northern Thai border town of Mae Sai. *Thai authorities.*

FIGURE 6 (ABOVE RIGHT). Industrial-scale *yaba* pill press seized by Thai authorities in Thailand's northern border town of Mae Sai. This pill compressor can manufacture approximately one hundred thousand pills per day and is the kind most commonly used in UWSA controlled methamphetamine "labs." *Thai authorities.*

FIGURE 7. Pill "punches" for *yaba* pill press. These elements of the compressor emboss the pills with, in this case, the WY brand marking which has established broad market recognition. *Thai authorities.*

FIGURE **8.** A statue of the lord Buddha pointing at Möng La's main stretch of casinos, nightclubs, and cabarets, which were effectively shut down in early 2005. *Michael Black.*

FIGURE **9.** A Hong Pang Company tollbooth on the road between Tachilek and Kengtung. *Michael Black.*

FIGURE 10 (TOP). Newly built casinos at Möng Ma, sixteen kilometers southwest of Möng La, Special Region 4. These were the first of the now fifty-two casinos to be operating in the area. Many offer online gambling. These first casinos were completed in April 2006. *Michael Black*.

FIGURE 11 (BOTTOM). Panoramic view of Möng La. *Milliam Couxeau.*

FIGURE 12 (ABOVE). A now defunct cabaret in Möng La which used to advertise erotic dancers from countries around the world. Next to it is a large nightclub. *Michael Black.*

FIGURE 13 (RIGHT). A sign outside one of Möng La's night clubs. *Michael Black.*

FIGURE 14. Chinese customs officials inspecting goods outbound from Möng La to southwestern Yunnan's town of Dalou.

FIGURE 15. Headquarters of Myanmar National Democratic Army Alliance (MNDAA) in Möng La. *Michael Black.*

FIGURE 16. The Oriental Hotel and Casino in Möng La is owned by Lin Mingxiang's wife with other Chinese investors. Construction was completed only a few months before Möng La was forced shut in early 2005. *Michael Black.*

FIGURE 17. United Wa State Army "Customs" troops on outskirts of Panghsang. *Jack Palitz.*

FIGURE 18. Storefronts on a Panghsang street. The lingua franca in Panghsang is Mandarin Chinese. However, Wa and other tribal languages and dialects are also spoken. *Jack Palitz.*

FIGURE 19. Chedi in Panghsang. The temple is adjacent to a Buddhist temple and Panghsang's central prison. *Jack Palitz.*

FIGURE 20. Statue of bull outside the Panghsang headquarters of the UWSA. In Wa culture the bull, namely its head, symbolizes strength and prosperity. *Jack Palitz.*

FIGURE 21 (LEFT). Brochure advertising a casino in Möng La.

FIGURE 22 (BELOW). Brochure advertising a casino in Möng La.

FIGURE 23 (TOP). UWSA troops training near Panghsang garrison. *Jack Palitz.*

FIGURE 24 (CENTER). A billboard in Panghsang exalts the UWSA. *Jack Palitz.*

FIGURE 25 (BOTTOM). One of many signs posted in and around Panghsang stating "No opium or any drug in Wa State. If you have any difficulties call an officer" with phone numbers. *Jack Palitz.*

FIGURE 26. Colonel Yawt Serk, commander of the Shan State Army South presiding over Shan resistance day festivities at SSA-S headquarters at Doi Taileng in Shan State across from Thailand's Mae Hong Son Province, May 21, 2006. *Michael Black.*

FIGURE 27. Entrance to Shan State Army South headquarters at Doi Taileng. Lettering in Shan and Thai languages welcomes visitors. *Michael Black.*

FIGURE 28. SSA-S regulars in early morning formation at the militia headquarters at Doi Taileng, southern Shan State, across from Thailand's Mae Hong Son Province. The soldier in the center appears to be a child. *Confidential source.*

FIGURE 29. SSA troops. *Confidential source.*

FIGURE 30. SSA-S soldier looks out over nearby UWSA positions at SSA-S forward position which saw a bloody UWSA-SPDC assault in April 2005. Many of the captured UWSA troops were high on methamphetamine while many of their less fortunate brothers in arms were found to be in the possession of *yaba* pills. *Michael Black.*

FIGURE 31. SSA-S commando troops at Doi Taileng headquarters across from Thailand's Mae Hong Son Province. *Confidential source.*

FIGURE 32. SSA-S commando troops in training drill at Doi Taileng headquarters north of Thailand's Mae Hong Son Province. *Confidential source.*

FIGURE 33. The 281-room hotel and casino at "Boten Golden City," Luang Namtha Province, Laos. The casino is owned by Lin Mingxiang and other Chinese investors. *Michael Black.*

FIGURE 34. Thailand's former prime minister, Thaksin Shinawatra, launched the "War against drugs" campaign in 2003.

FIGURE 35. Thailand anti-drug campaign poster.

THREE

SMACK AND SPEED

CONTRARY TO popular belief, the Golden Triangle has not always been a major drug-producing area—nor has the sale and consumption of opium always been illegal. Prior to World War II, all countries in Southeast Asia had government-controlled opium monopolies, not unlike the tobacco monopolies today. What was illegal was to smuggle opium and to trade without a license. Most local addicts were ethnic Chinese, who had migrated to Southeast Asia's urban centers in the nineteenth and early twentieth centuries—and brought with them the opium smoking habit from their old homes in China.

In the beginning, Thailand (then Siam) had actually tried to stop the practice. In 1811 King Rama II had promulgated Siam's first formal ban on selling and consuming opium. In 1839, King Rama III reiterated the prohibition and introduced the death penalty for major opium traffickers. These efforts, however, were doomed to failure. Ethnic Chinese traffickers could be arrested and punished—but a much more powerful institution was pushing Siam to open its doors to the drug: the British East India Company, which had initiated large-scale cultivation in its Indian colonies and was looking for new export markets in the region.

Siam was never a colony, but that did not mean that it escaped the scourges that had followed foreign rule in neighboring countries. Finally, in 1852, Siam's revered King Mongkut (Rama IV) bowed to British pressure. He established a royal opium franchise which was farmed out to local entrepreneurs, mostly wealthy Chinese traders. Opium, lottery, gambling, and alcohol permits were up for grabs. By the end of the nineteenth century, taxes on these monopolies provided between 40 and 50 percent of Siam's government revenue.

But despite the ready market for opium, there was surprisingly little poppy cultivation in Thailand until the 1940s. The royal monopoly imported expensive opium from India and the Middle East, and continued to do so until the government-licensed drug trade was abolished in 1959. Some cheaper opium was also smuggled in from China, where large-scale poppy cultivation had begun in the mid-nineteenth century. For not even in China is the opium poppy actually an indigenous crop; it was first introduced there by Arab traders in the seventh and eighth centuries. It became popular immediately, but was not cultivated commercially to any significant extent until about 150 years ago.

The opium poppy (*papaver somniferum*) was first discovered sometime in the Neolithic Age, growing wild in the mountains bordering the eastern Mediterranean. Ancient medical chronicles show that raw opium, scraped off the pods of the poppies, was highly regarded by early physicians hundreds of years before the Christian Era. It was known to Hippocrates in ancient Greece; during the time of the Roman Empire, it was known to the great physician Galen. From its original home in what today is Afyon (hence "opium") in Turkey, opium spread westward to the Balkan peninsula—and eastward to India and China.

Opium was first used as a medicine in China more than a thousand years ago, but its soothing effects on the user soon turned it into what today is called a recreational drug, and some users began smoking instead of eating it. The Spaniards had learned the habit of smoking tobacco in South America, and they brought this custom with them to their East Asian colony, the Philippines. Smoking spread from there to China in the early seventeenth century. Meanwhile, the Dutch in Formosa (now Taiwan) had learned to smoke a mixture of opium and tobacco to combat the effects of malaria—and some Chinese acquired this habit as well.

Gradually, some of those who smoked began to eliminate the tobacco from the blend. Opium as a stimulant had been discovered. Yet the reasons for smoking varied considerably. For the rich it was primarily a luxury, used in the same way that affluent people today snort cocaine at fashionable parties or take ecstasy before going to discotheques. Cheaper, diluted versions of opium helped the poor escape from their daily miseries, as heroin mixed with glucose or *yaba* does in Bangkok's Klong Toey and other slums today.

Although small amounts of raw opium were harvested in the Golden Triangle in the eighteenth and nineteenth centuries, India was the main producer of the drug for international trading. Some of India's Mughal emperors tried to tax opium sales to raise revenue for the state. No single organization in any part of Asia, however, had the will, the networks, or the political and naval clout to create new markets before the advent of the colonial powers.

Britain's move to colonize India and other parts of Asia heralded a new era in international opium trading. In 1600, the East India Company had been formed with the aim of expanding trade contacts between Britain and Asia, and between British spheres of influence in the Far East. In subsequent centuries this trade was pursued with much vigor. The stalwart mariners and traders of the East India Company fought their way into the highly competitive markets of Asia, followed by the armies of Britain's expanding colonial empire.

China, with its teeming millions of people, held the greatest attraction. It seemed likely to be a great market for the products of the growing British Empire; and, more importantly, China could supply goods that were becoming popular in Europe itself—especially tea. Britain, however, faced severe problems in its trade relations with China. At first, the British had little to offer that the Chinese wanted. In fact, the Chinese showed interest in only one item from Britain and British India: silver. By the late eighteenth century, the cargo of every British ship that sailed from India to Guangzhou (Canton) was 90 percent silver bullion.

By the early nineteenth century India faced a shortage of silver, and another commodity had to be found. The answer was opium, which grew in abundance in India and was gradually becoming popular in China. Opium replaced silver as the currency of trade with the Chinese. The flow of silver from India to China was effectively halted, and after the mid-nineteenth century the silver trade completely reversed direction. Silver was now going back to India from China to pay for opium. India had also begun its own tea production, and the loser in this game was China. India's income from the Chinese opium trade paid for constructing grand imperial buildings in Calcutta, Madras, Bombay, and other cities established by the British. An opium tax soon produced more than one-fifth of government revenue in the vast empire of British India.

But Britain was far from being China's only opium supplier. Americans also sold Turkish opium to the Chinese. Clipper ships belonging to well-respected firms such as Perkins & Company and Russell & Company of Boston transported immense quantities of opium from the Middle East to China. Persian opium was later imported by any trader in a position to do so. The American merchant W.C. Hunter used one simple phrase to describe the Chinese opium trade between 1835 and 1844: "We were all equally implicated."

The Chinese government tried, at least officially, to suppress the trade. Opium was devastating China's population as millions of people became addicted to the drug. Opium smoking had actually been prohibited in China in 1729; cultivating and importing opium was specifically banned in 1799. But these edicts were ignored by all Western merchants—and the ruling Qing, or Manchu, Dynasty was too weak to enforce its policies. Moreover, local officials were too corrupt to obey orders from the court in Beijing, or unwilling to follow directives from a dynasty of foreign emperors who originated in Manchuria.

The Qing emperors tried time and again to stop the inflow of opium and the outflow of hard currency. Then, in March 1839, Emperor Xuan-zong appointed an unusually vigorous official, Lin Zexu, as commissioner for foreign trade and sent him down to Guangzhou to stamp out the opium business. Lin demanded that the merchants sign bonds promising never to bring opium to China again, on pain of death. Some American merchants signed, but the British refused. In a series of letters to Queen Victoria, commissioner Lin appealed to the British to stop the trade. There was no response, and Lin wrote in a final, carefully worded letter to the Queen:

> Let us suppose that foreigners came from another country and brought opium into England, and seduced the people of your country to smoke it. Would you not, the sovereign of the said country, look upon such a procedure with anger, and in your just indignation endeavor to get rid of it? Now we have always heard that Your Highness possesses a most kind and benevolent heart. Surely then you are incapable of doing or causing to be done unto another that which you should not wish another to do unto you.

Moral persuasion has never proved very effective in dealing with drug smuggling or the rulers who sanction it, and the British in Guangzhou were no exception. When diplomacy did not help, Lin decided to use force. In June he destroyed twenty thousand chests of opium weighing 133 pounds each, which had been seized from foreign merchants' warehouses. Lord Palmerston, the British foreign secretary, decided to retaliate: a powerful fleet, with four thousand soldiers aboard, was assembled. An official proclamation said that the fleet would "protect British interests." Admiral George Elliot was in charge of the overall operation, with Vice-Admiral Sir William Parker and military commander Sir Henry Gough sailing with the warships.

High-powered British naval cannons bombarded the ports along the South China Sea to force the Emperor to open them to British merchandise—which was primarily opium from India. The British fleet laid siege to Guangzhou, took Amoy (Xiamen) and Ningbo, and finally occupied Shanghai in July 1842, cutting off supplies to Beijing, which were delivered via the Grand Canal, a massive, ancient man-made waterway that connected the Yellow River—the Huanghe—with the Yangzi. China was defeated, and on August 29 the first treaty was signed with Britain on board the Cornwallis. Known as the Treaty of Nanjing, it required that the Chinese pay twenty-one million silver dollars in reparations, open five ports—including Shanghai—to British trade, and cede the island of Hong Kong to Queen Victoria. The new colony of Hong Kong gave the British a tremendous advantage over other opium merchants. Trade with China became a virtual British monopoly, and Hong Kong emerged as the most important transfer point for Indian opium entering the vast Chinese market. By 1854, yearly British sales of opium amounted to nearly eighty thousand chests, and China's opium smokers numbered in the millions.

The opium trade, organized from Hong Kong and Shanghai, laid the foundation for many personal fortunes. The most successful entrepreneurs of all were two young Britons: William Jardine and James Matheson. Veteran Australian journalist Richard Hughes described them as "both Scottish, both religious in the stiff Calvinist way, both scrupulous in financial and personal matters, both indifferent to moralistic reflections on contraband and drugs." Jardine-Matheson went on to become one of the biggest trading firms in Shanghai, and remains so in Hong Kong. Its present-day executives are conventional members of the Hong Kong business world, and few of them would like to be reminded of how their company's wealth and influence originated.

Frictions between the Chinese and the foreigners continued after the acquisition of Hong Kong and the opening of Shanghai to foreign trade. A second opium war was fought from 1856 to 1860. China lost again, and more territory was ceded to the British. The Kowloon Peninsula was added to the British colony of Hong Kong—and the British also proposed the legalisation of the opium trade, to which the Chinese reluctantly agreed. According to the terms of the new agreement, "the importer was to sell [opium] only at the port. It was to be carried to the interior by Chinese only. . . . and the transit dues were to be arranged as the Chinese government saw fit."

But this was on paper only. Opium continued to be the most important commodity that foreigners traded with China. Following its military defeats, the Chinese were too weak, and local officials too corrupt, to stop the drug flow into their country. Britain continued to export increasing amounts of Indian opium. In the peak year of 1880, China imported more than 6,500 tons, most of which was produced in India. But then, in the 1860s, China began to grow her own on a massive scale. After 1880 the demand for foreign opium decreased, and by 1905 imported opium amounted to roughly half the amount of 1880. By the early twentieth century, China's own annual opium production had risen to twenty-two thousand tons, providing drugs for at least fifteen million addicts and many more occasional users.

The areas of China most suitable for growing the opium poppy were in Sichuan and, most importantly, in Yunnan, which was then bordered by British Burma and French Indochina: the protectorates of Laos and Tongkin (now northern Vietnam). This mountainous region was high enough to grow the opium poppy. It had also become the home of various hill tribes, ethnically distinct from both the Chinese to the north and the lowland peoples of Southeast Asia. Some tribes—such as the Karens and various Mon-Khmer speaking hill peoples—had been living in the highlands of northern Thailand, Laos, and Vietnam for centuries, even before the plains people arrived. But political instability in southern China in the nineteenth and early twentieth century had forced the southward migration of many more hill peoples such as the Hmong, the Yao, the Lahu, the Lisu, and the Akha.

The opium poppy soon became a valuable cash crop for those hilltribe refugees. It could earn two to four times the income of wheat grown on the same amount of land. In the late nineteenth century, poppy cultivation spread from Yunnan into northeastern Burma, and to the hill country of northern parts of Thailand and French Indochina—which also led to the establishment of opium monopolies in all those territories, although most of the drug continued to be imported from India and the Middle East.

At an early stage, the French had turned to opium to finance their conquest of Indochina. The cities of Hanoi, Hue, and Saigon already had large opium-smoking populations—primarily of the Chinese merchant class—and they were initially supplied with opium imported from China. Once in power, the French licensed several opium trading houses, which all operated according to the same rules. Merchants paid a tax to the colonial government on opium both bought in the hills of Laos and Tongkin, and imported from India and the Middle East. The drug was then sold to local consumers through shops or in opium smoking parlors.

In the late nineteenth century the various French drug interests were consolidated under a single government-administered opium monopoly: a powerful agency called the *Régie de l'Opium*. Profits soared and trade was brisk. By 1900, tax on opium accounted for more than half of all revenues in French Indochina. In 1930, the territory had 3,500 licensed opium dens, or one for every 1,500 adult males. Drug abuse had spread from the upper strata of society down to coolies in the ports.

In Burma the situation was entirely different. The old Burmese kingdom had been conquered in stages from 1826 to 1885 and made a province of British India. Between Britain's new colony and French Indochina lay Thailand, or Siam, which survived as an independent buffer state between the two colonial powers. But to the north of Thailand—and between Burma, Yunnan, and French Indochina—was an area too politically and ethnically diverse to become a separately run buffer territory. These were the rugged Shan hills, where hill tribes lived in the highlands and rice-growing, Buddhist Shans—cousins of the Thais and the Lao—populated the fertile river valleys. But unlike the Thais, the Shans had no unified kingdom. They were ruled by dozens of different princes, and in order to "pacify" this uncontrollable and potentially dangerous hill country, the British conquest was extended up into the Shan hills. By 1890, this area was also brought under British rule. However, the thirty-or-so Shan principalities were declared protectorates, and not made part of Burma proper. The princes were allowed to retain their titles, and were left more or less alone—as long as peace prevailed in their tiny states.

Small quantities of opium—before World War II perhaps thirty tons or so per year—were grown in these highlands, and opium taxes produced some income for the Shan princes. But the cultivation was restricted to some remote hill areas east of the Salween river: Kokang, a district dominated by ethnic Chinese, and the wild Wa Hills, where people were headhunters well into modern times. The trade was strictly controlled by the colonial authorities under the 1910 Opium Act and later by the 1938 Opium Rules.

Opium was a state monopoly, and a resident excise officer was stationed at each vendor's shop to supervise sales and to verify that surplus opium was discarded every evening. A British government report from 1909 stated:

> Licenses are allotted to selected vendors at a fixed fee and the profits are determined by the difference between the wholesale rate at which opium is issued from the Treasury and the retail price at which the vendor is required to sell to customers . . . the receipts are growing steadily but do not yet cover expenditure.

So opium use was not that widespread. In fact, there is only one reference to opium in the main pre-war anthropological study of the Shans, written in 1910 by Leslie Milne: "No religious Shan takes opium, so it is not openly used as a medicine, but native doctors use it occasionally mixed with herbs."

The situation was under much less control in China. In London, Christians and liberals argued intensely and emotionally that the opium trade from British India was immoral. Their efforts had succeeded in 1917, when India's opium exports to China were banned. But by then many Chinese warlords were already encouraging China's hill tribes to cultivate poppies so that an opium tax could pay for their troops. The emperor in Beijing had been overthrown by a revolution in 1911–12, and something approaching civil war was raging in many parts of China.

The collapse of the millennia-old Chinese empire brought chaos and rivalry between several new, republican contenders for power. And the seeds of future conflict had already been planted—not only in southern China, but also in the remote highlands of Southeast Asia's Golden Triangle.

THE POST-WORLD WAR II OPIUM BOOM

World War II altered not only the political map of Asia—independence for India in 1947 eventually led to the end of colonial rule in the world's most populous continent—but also had a dramatic impact on Southeast Asia's opium trade. Touby Ly Fong, chief of the Hmong tribe in Laos and an official in the French *Régie de l'Opium* between 1939 and 1945, described how the war affected Laos:

> Before World War II, the French government bought opium in Afghanistan and India, and warehoused it at Hanoi. During the war, when they could no longer import it, they encouraged local poppy-growing so that the Chinese, the Vietnamese and French smokers in the colony could still get their supplies. The Lao themselves have never smoked much. The crop was grown mainly by Hmong tribes and the Yaos, and to some extent by the Lahus and the Lisus.

At first, the French tried to deal directly with the producers, which failed because payment could not be made until the French knew the morphine content of the opium, which could take several weeks. The impoverished hilltribe growers could not wait that long, so the French employed middlemen, usually Chinese merchants who had some capital and were able to advance money. These brokers paid for the opium in cash, making sure that there was a handsome margin between the price they paid the peasants and the payment they received from the French authorities. The middlemen grew rich on the deal—but the hill tribes remained as poor as they had ever been.

On average, the French bought forty tons of opium a year from these middlemen in Laos. The consumers were to be found in Hanoi, Saigon, Vientiane, and other lowland cities. Only in the French-protected kingdom of Cambodia was there very little drug abuse. Cambodia was too flat, hot, and humid to grow its own opium—although some was imported and sold through government-licensed opium dens in the capital Phnom Penh. In the wake of the war, the mountains of northern Laos and northwestern Tongkin (now northern Vietnam) took over from India and the Middle East as the main supplier of opium to consumers all over French Indochina.

In Burma, the sleepy and stagnant *Pax Britannica* came to an abrupt end when the Japanese overran and occupied the country in 1942. Fierce battles were fought in the Shan hills between the Japanese Imperial Army and Nationalist Chinese Kuomintang (KMT) units, invited by the Allies and dispatched by Chiang Kai-shek's commanders in Yunnan. The Allies and the Japanese each in turn bombed Shan towns and the country descended into a state of chaos and destruction.

Alongside the Japanese fought the Burmese nationalists, organized in the Burma Independence Army (BIA) and commanded by Aung San, a charismatic young personality often referred to as "the George Washington of Burma." One year before the Japanese invasion a group of thirty young Burmese, known as "The Thirty Comrades," had secretly left Burma to get military training on the Japanese-controlled Chinese island of Hainan. They had been taken in by the Japanese war cry, "Asia to the Asians!" Meanwhile, the Kachin and the Karen, as well as some other ethnic minorities, organized guerrilla forces that fought against the Japanese. Support came from the British and the Americans, who also send special operatives to fight alongside the minority peoples.

However, the BIA was not allowed to enter the Shan States or any other frontier areas. The Japanese, like the British before them, treated the Shan States as a separate political entity. They even handed over the biggest of them, Kengtung (32,000 sq. km.), along with the smaller state of Möng

Pan (7,700 sq. km.), to Thailand, which was allied with Japan during the war. Later, when the group led by Aung San realized that Japan was interested only in a puppet regime in Burma, the BIA contacted its former enemies, the British, and the Burmese nationalists were reorganized into the Anti-Fascist People's Freedom League (AFPFL). The Burmese nationalists, now backed by the British, took up arms against the Japanese on March 27, 1945—after the Kachin had held their festival to celebrate their victory in the war in the far north, and the Karen were chasing fleeing Japanese troops down to the lowlands. Since then, however, March 27 has been commemorated as Armed Forces Day in Burma, much to the chagrin of many of the minority peoples.

These tactical mistakes of the Burmese nationalist movement during the war widened the gap between the Burmese and the various frontier peoples, who were, generally speaking, more pro-British than the Burmese. Many minority peoples—notably the Karens and the Kachins—who had fought against the Japanese throughout the occupation distrusted the Burmese nationalists, whom they viewed as collaborators. Many Karens had been butchered by overzealous BIA units, further deepening mistrust of the Burmese nationalist movement.

When British rule was restored after the war, Aung San and his nationalists carried on their struggle for independence. The process might have taken a longer time had it not been for the political upheaval in neighboring India. In 1947 it was clear that India was going to become independent—and the British saw no reason to cling on to Burma, which as a colony had been first part of, and later ancillary to, the British possessions in India. On January 27, 1947, Aung San and the British Labor prime minister, Clement Attlee, signed an agreement that would give independence to Burma the following year. But what shape independence would take was still unclear. When Aung San attended a meeting with the British in London, the Shan princes sent a telegram to Attlee stating that he was representing the Burmese only, and not the frontier peoples.

Despite the difficulties, the leaders of the Shan, Kachin, and Chin peoples met a few weeks later at the market town of Panglong, north of Loi Lem in the Shan States. They also invited Aung San, and an agreement was signed in which the hill peoples agreed to join a proposed Union of Burma provided they were granted local autonomy within their respective areas. The day when the Panglong Agreement was signed, February 12, has since then been officially celebrated in Burma as Union Day, a national holiday. The Shan princes also asked for, and were granted, the right to secede from the proposed Union of Burma, should they be dissatisfied with the new federation. This right was ensured under the first Burmese constitution.

But discussions with other, smaller tribes were more difficult. The head-hunting Was had their own views on a union with Burma. In some areas they had adopted the Shan system of *saohpas*, and a few local chieftains called themselves "princes" of "Wa States." But the hearings before the commission that was looking into the aspirations of the frontier peoples revealed a wide gap between the British or Burmese way and the Wa perception of life and society. Questions were asked by the chairman of the commission and answered by two Wa chieftains, Hkun Sai of Mongkong and Sao Maha of Vingngun:

> *Do you want any association with other people?*
> —We do not want to join anybody because in the past we have been very independent.

> *What do you want the future to be of the Wa States?*
> —We have not thought about that because we are wild people. We never thought of the administrative future. We only think about ourselves.

> *Don't you want education, clothing, good food, good houses, hospitals etc.?*
> —We are very wild people and we do not appreciate all these things.

During colonial times, British imperial presence in the Wa Hills was limited to annual flag marches up to the Chinese frontier. But even that could be hazardous, as many of the soldiers in the British contingents were of Indian origin—and, as the Shan writer Sao Saimong related in his *The Shan States and the British Annexation*: "During the Wa States tour of a British officer in 1939, a Sikh doctor had to be rushed out of the head-hunting area under en escort of a platoon of troops when it was learned that the Wa came and offered three hundred silver rupees to some of his camp followers for this head which, with its magnificent beard and moustache, they said would bring enduring prosperity to their village."

The British never even tried to exercise effective control over the Wa Hills, and the situation after the defeat of the Japanese remained the same. The Was were left alone, and never considered themselves part of a larger entity called Burma.

On paper, everything was ready for the declaration of the independence of the Union of Burma—which was going to take place at the auspicious hour of dawn on January 4, 1948—when an event occurred that was as unexpected as it was tragic. On July 19, 1947, the Burmese nation was shocked by the message that Aung San had been assassinated, along with eight of his closest associates. The state of affairs when Burma achieved its independence in 1948 could hardly have been worse. The country had suffered some of the most severe air strikes in Asia during the war; the countryside was ravaged and the infrastructure almost destroyed. The inner circle of competent leaders had been murdered even before independence had been proclaimed. The new leader and independent Burma's first prime minister, U Nu, was a talented, intellectual politician but hardly the strong statesman Burma needed during its first, difficult years of independence. Army units rose in mutiny, the Karen minority took up arms and demanded a separate state, and the communists went underground to organize guerrilla forces.

In an attempt to forge national unity, the Shan leader Sao Shwe Thaike—the prince of Yawnghwe state—had been given the ceremonial post of the first President of the Union of Burma. But events in the Shan States thwarted such attempts to placate the increasingly restless hill peoples.

Following the victory of Mao Zedong's communists, and the proclamation of their People's Republic of China on October 1, 1949, Chiang Kai-shek's main KMT force retreated to Taiwan, where his Republic of China lived on after the loss of the mainland. Fighting continued for several months in some remote parts of China, including Yunnan, but the communists emerged victorious even there. In January 1950, hundreds of defeated KMT forces from Yunnan—unable to withstand the attacks of the Chinese communists, and also unable to join Chiang Kai-shek's main force on the island of Taiwan—crossed over into Shan territory in northeastern Burma. Later led by wartime hero General Li Mi, they in effect invaded the mountains of Kengtung and also ensconced themselves in the hilly region surrounding Möng Hsat, close to the Thai border as well as parts of the Wa Hills.

The KMT forces in the Shan hills contacted Taiwan through its embassy in Bangkok—and it was decided not to evacuate them to Taiwan but to turn the Nationalist Chinese soldiers in the Shan hills into a "liberation army" that would build up bases in northeastern Burma and from there try to retake China from the communists. The tiny Möng Hsat airstrip, built during World War II, was reconstructed into a formidable air base, capable of receiving C-46 and C-47 transport planes, which brought in arms, ammunition, and medical supplies. The KMT also recruited new soldiers from the border areas—mostly Lahu hilltribesmen—and gave them military training. The Kengtung-based "secret" KMT army tried on no less than seven occasions between 1950 and 1952 to invade Yunnan, but was repeatedly driven back into the Shan States.

The Burmese army was sent to the Shan States to rid the country of its uninvited guests—but was unsuccessful. U Nu then raised the question in the United Nations General Assembly, which on April 22, 1953, adopted a resolution demanding that the KMT lay down its arms and leave the country. Thousands of KMT soldiers were evacuated with pomp and circumstance to Taiwan by special aircraft—at the same time as reinforcements were being flown in to Möng Hsat by nightly flights. Thus, the number of KMT soldiers in the Shan States increased to twelve thousand by the end of 1953.

The Burmese army failed to defeat them, but managed to drive some of the units across the Salween river into the Wa Hills and Kokang, traditionally the best opium growing areas of the Shan States. The KMT had become involved in the Golden Triangle opium trade earlier on, but they were now able to trade more directly. They enlisted the support of Olive Yang (Yang Jinxiu or Yang Kyin-hsui), the leader of the ethnic Chinese district of Kokang. Known locally as "Miss Hairy Legs," this unfeminine woman, still in her early twenties, came to command her own army of nearly one thousand men.

Like so many other children of aristocratic Shan States families, Olive Yang had attended the prestigious Guardian Angel's Convent School in

Lashio. Former classmates remembered that their parents warned them not to play with the odd little girl: "Stay away from Olive!" they used to say. "She's got a revolver in her schoolbag."

When Olive finished her education she no longer had to hide her gun. She was formally proclaimed ruling princess of Kokang and went about the district in a gray uniform, with a Belgian army pistol on each hip. Backed by the KMT, Olive became the first warlord—or perhaps one should say warlady—to send opium by convoys of trucks instead of mules down to the Thai border. On these occasions, heavily armed Kokang troops—called "Olive's boys"—lined the roads to provide security. This is the same "warlady" who in 1989 played an important role in negotiating the cease-fire agreements between Burma's military government and the former CPB forces.

The money she earned from these operations was used to arm and equip her army—and to buy lavish gifts for her lover, the famous Burmese film actress Wa Wa Win Shwe. Olive's troops traded with the KMT, and their armed support added to the general instability of the frontier areas. This kept the Burmese Army occupied and split up on several different fronts, which benefited the KMT. The Nationalist Chinese involvement in the Golden Triangle opium trade was openly explained by one of the KMT's most famous generals, Duan Xiwen:

> We have to continue to fight the evil of communism and to fight you must have an army, and an army must have guns, and to buy guns you must have money. In these mountains, the only money is opium.

This statement prophetically described why so many other armed groups in the Shan States—including the Burmese government's own army and local militia forces—would become involved in the complex politics of the Golden Triangle drug trade. To this very day, the situation remains the same.

To finance its secret war against Mao Zedong's communists in China, the KMT turned to almost the only cash crop of any significance in the Shan hills: opium. In 1950, when the KMT first entered the area, the annual production there amounted to a mere thirty tons. But the KMT persuaded the hilltribe farmers to grow more opium; they introduced a hefty opium tax that forced the farmers to grow even more in order to make ends meet. By the mid-1950s, opium production in the Burmese sector of the Golden Triangle had shot up ten to twenty times, to an annual yield of three hundred to four hundred tons. And more sons of the hilltribe farmers were recruited to fight for a cause they knew little about.

The KMT conducted a reign of terror from its strongholds in the Shan hills. According to Elaine T. Lewis, an American missionary who was working in Kengtung state in the 1950s:

> For many years, there have been large numbers of Chinese nationalist troops in the area demanding food and money from the local people. The areas in which these troops operate are getting poorer and some villagers are finding it necessary to flee.

Thousands of hilltribe villagers, mainly Akha from the hills north of Kengtung close to the Chinese frontier where the KMT had its secret bases, left their homes and settled in Chiang Rai province in northern Thailand, where they still remain. Many Lahus also migrated to Thailand, which already had a fairly substantial Lahu population in the northern hills.

The KMT effort in the Golden Triangle also involved the US Central Intelligence Agency: this was the first in a series of clandestine CIA operations against undesirable regimes in the Third World, and it was later to be followed by similar missions in Tibet, Laos, the Congo, Angola, Afghanistan, Cambodia, and Nicaragua. In fact, institutions and individuals who were later prominent in other covert operations got their first experience and training in the Golden Triangle. The best known of them was Colonel Paul Helliwell, who operated the local transport company that flew supplies from Thailand to the KMT in Möng Hsat. In the late 1950s, he moved to Miami where he became an important figure in the failed Bay of Pigs invasion and other CIA battles against Cuba's Fidel Castro.

The secret war in the Golden Triangle was also a failure. The KMT's forces and special agents could not ignite any rebellion in Yunnan, and, frustrated, they increasingly turned their attention to the more lucrative opium trade. The secret war may have had little influence on China, but the KMT's and the CIA's covert operations in the Golden Triangle resulted in large-scale poppy cultivation all over Burma's northern mountains.

The KMT invasion, combined with the government's inability to repel the invaders, meant that the Shans—and the hill tribes as well—became squeezed between two forces, both of which were perceived as foreign. The KMT was conducting a reign of terror from its mountain strongholds—but, on the other hand, reports were reaching Rangoon that the government forces had been no better in their treatment of the village people in the Shan countryside.

Shan students at Rangoon University began to organize a movement which sought to strengthen Shan culture and literature—and which also became increasingly antagonistic towards the government's army. The Burmese government viewed this development with unease, especially since the constitutional right to secede from the Union would come into effect in 1958. It tried to suppress the fledgling Shan nationalist movement by using the army and its Military Intelligence Service (MIS), but the outcome was counterproductive: groups of young Shans moved into the jungle, where they organized armed guerrilla units. In 1959 the first battles took place between the government's forces and the Shan rebels.

Attempts were made to solve the crisis by political means. In 1959 the Shan princes renounced all their powers at a grand ceremony in Taung-gyi—and their duties were taken over by a democratically elected Shan government. The Shan States became Shan State, and a movement also began to try to save the Union by strengthening its federal character. U Nu was willing to listen, and in February 1962 the Burmese government convened the Nationalities' Seminar in Rangoon in order to discuss the future status of the frontier areas, or the Constituent States, as they were now called. All the government ministers, members of parliament, heads of the constituent states (at that time Shan State, Kachin State, Karenni or Kayah State, and Karen State), and their state ministers attended this seminar.

But on March 2, 1962, before any decision had been taken, the chief of the army, General Ne Win, staged his coup d'état and detained all the participants of the meeting. He also abolished the old federal constitution and introduced military rule headed by a revolutionary council, with himself as chairman. The Shan leader Sao Shwe Thaike was arrested and died in prison a few months later. Another prominent Shan prince, Sao Kya Hseng of Hsipaw, was also taken away by the army and never seen again.

The army claimed that it had to intervene to "save the Union from disintegration." But, instead, rebellions flared anew in Shan State—and new rebel armies emerged in Kachin State and many other parts of the country. Burma's frontier areas were plunged into chaos—and as a result opium production began to increase even more dramatically.

THE BURMESE WAY TO RUIN

The most pressing problem the new insurgent armies in northeastern Burma's frontier areas had to face was finding financial backing for their armed struggle against Burma's new military government. With no external support, funds had to be raised from the resources of their own respective areas. The Kachin rebels quickly gained control over the jade-mining district around Hpakan in western Kachin State. But in Shan State there was no similar source of income for the insurgents. One commodity, however, was already well established at the beginning of the rebellion and could bring in cash: opium. Although the actual trade remained in the hands of well-connected ethnic Chinese businessmen, the rebels controlled the countryside where the poppies were grown and were thus able to tax the business.

The KMT invasion and the devastation of the countryside had severely damaged the rice-based economy of Shan State. Farmers had to become porters for the government troops conducting offensives against the insurgents. Many of them left their paddy fields and took to the hills, where the opium poppy was the only viable crop they could grow—and the demand for the drug was increasing steadily. The poppy had previously been cultivated by the hill tribes and the Kokang Chinese; now many impoverished Shan farmers also took up opium farming.

Furthermore, up to the mid-1960s only opium was traded in the Golden Triangle, but the war and the chaos in the frontier areas now enabled private armies run by local warlords to carve out their own bailiwicks where their troops protected a new phenomenon: laboratories where raw opium was refined into morphine and, later, heroin. In the beginning, raw opium from the Golden Triangle was smuggled on board Chinese fishing boats and junks from the Thai coast to Hong Kong, where it was refined into heroin in clandestine laboratories in remote areas of the colony. But following several crackdowns by the British police, the production of heroin had to be relocated closer to the source.

Southeast Asia's first heroin refineries were established in the mid-1960s in the hills near Ban Huay Xai in Laos, across the Mekong river from Chiang Khong in Thailand. Later, new refineries were established on the Thai-Burmese border as well. Skilled chemists were brought in from Hong Kong and Taiwan, and enormous profits were made from the trade in this, for Southeast Asia, new, expensive, and very dangerous drug. "Smack," as it became known among addicts, found its way into the slums of Bangkok—and beyond. Much higher prices for the drug in the United States and Australia led to the creation of worldwide smuggling networks, which reaped enormous profits on the misery of the addicts.

The economic policies of General Ne Win also contributed to the rise in drug production that occurred in the mid- and late-1960s. His "revolutionary council" announced that the country now had to follow a new ideology called the "Burmese Way to Socialism." Its effects on the opium trade have been described by Chao Tzang Yawnghwe, one of the sons of Shan leader and first president of Burma, Sao Shwe Thaike:

The fast rolling opium bandwagon was further oiled by the introduction of the Burmese Way to Socialism following General Ne Win's coup of 1962. All businesses and banks (foreign and otherwise), shops, industries, factories, etc., were nationalized, and business and trade by individuals and private concerns came to a dead stop. Naturally, in such an economic vacuum there arose a black market economy, which for the opium traffickers was a boon as they, and only they, were equipped to exploit this sad situation. Opium was bought by them at very low price from ragged cultivators, transported in armed caravans to the [Thai] border and refined into heroin. And on the return trip to get more opium, Thai goods and commodities were taken up and sold in Shan State at very high prices—thus a killing was made both ways, at least thrice yearly. Rather than creating socialism, the Burmese Way to Socialism in effect delivered the economy into the hands of the opium traffickers. As such, opium became the only viable crop and medium of exchange. Thus, cultivation of opium, limited to east of the Salween river prior to 1963, not only spread all over Shan State, but to Kachin, Karenni and Chin states as well.

Within a few years of this disastrous experiment with "socialism," more than 80 percent of all consumer goods available in Burma were smuggled in from neighboring countries, primarily Thailand. Opium—and increasingly heroin—became the medium of exchange, as the Burmese kyat had become worthless for trading with other countries.

The 1962 coup and the escalation of warfare threw Shan State into anarchy. The situation deteriorated even further when China, long wary of the unpredictable general in power in Rangoon, decided to lend open support to its Burmese sister party, the Communist Party of Burma (CPB). Apart from a desire to spread revolutionary ideology to Burma, there was also another reason why China had decided to support the CPB: the revitalized People's Army of Burma smashed all the KMT's old bases in northeastern Shan State, from where they had been able to conduct cross-border raids and intelligence-gathering forays into Yunnan. The KMT was forced to retreat down to the Thai border, where they reached an understanding with the Thai authorities. They acted as a buffer and unofficial border police, and sent soldiers to protect road construction crews in sensitive areas in Thailand where the Communist Party of Thailand (CPT) was active. Some KMT units even participated actively in counterinsurgency campaigns against CPT strongholds in Thailand.

On the Thai border, the KMT was reorganised into the third and fifth regiments, commanded by General Li Wenhuan and General Duan Xiwen respectively. Even before the CPB's takeover of Kokang, the Wa Hills and the area north of Kengtung, General Li had established his headquarters at Tam Ngob, northwest of Chiang Mai, and General Duan at Mae Salong further to the north. But as the importance of the KMT grew along the border so too did these previously relatively small base camps. Mae Salong, especially, developed into a prosperous town with shops, restaurants, and even tourist resorts.

Both the third and the fifth KMT regiments established "tax stations" along the border, where they collected "customs duty" on opium convoys reaching Thai territory. Inside Shan State, they operated through allies working on their behalf. In 1964, several Shan rebel groups had united under one banner—the Shan State Army (SSA)—first headed by Sao Nang Hearn Kham, the widow of Sao Shwe Thaike. The SSA remained fiercely opposed to the KMT—its terror was one of the reasons why the Shans had taken up arms in the first place—but one of her men, Mo Heing, broke away to set up his own Shan United Revolutionary Army (SURA). This group found sanctuary at Pieng Luang on the Thai border west of Chiang Dao, an area which was under General Li's unofficial jurisdiction.

Then came the Ka Kwe Ye home guard program, launched by Burma's military intelligence apparatus, which took over much of the trade from the KMT. In this truly confused imbroglio, it soon became impossible to say where drug-running ended, and insurgency, counterinsurgency and espionage began. By the late 1960s, the components of the emerging opium hierarchy could be described in this way:

The farmers who grew the poppies earned a pittance for months of laborious work. They were mostly hill tribes, such as Kachin, Lahu, Wa, Lisu, Palaung, and Akha, but there were also poor, ethnic Chinese peasants from Kokang and other areas in the hills east of Kutkai and Hsenwi in northeastern Shan State. Despite living at subsistence level, they had to pay "taxes" to various rebel groups claiming their areas, and bribes to various government officials who were supposed to enforce the law.

The rebels who operated in the poppy growing areas collected tax from the farmers, but the most politically motivated of the groups, the Shan State Army (SSA), was never involved to any appreciable extent in the opium business. No more than one thousand *viss*, or roughly 1.5 tons, was grown in the SSA area south of the Hsenwi-Lashio road and north of Kehsi Mansam. This harvest was less than 0.2 percent of all the opium produced in Shan State at that time. The SSA nevertheless levied a 10 percent opium tax on the growers, another 10 percent on the buyers, and an additional tax for traders and caravans passing through their territory. Opium tax paid for the rebels' arms purchases in Thailand and Laos.

The merchants who bought the opium from the farmers and paid tax to the rebels were—and still are—respectable local businessmen who live quite openly in government-controlled market towns. They sent their agents to the hills to purchase opium and then used various armed bands to transport the drugs to the refineries along the Thai border or in Laos. The front for a middleman operation like this could be an ordinary trading house, doubling as a wholesaler of potatoes, pork, or consumer goods.

The Ka Kwe Ye (KKY), Burma's once infamous home guard units, were often hired by the merchants to convey the drugs. Many KKY commanders were also merchants themselves. If local militia bosses like Lo Hsing-han or Khun Sa, for instance, conducted a convoy down to the Thai border, they would be carrying their own opium as well as drugs belonging to other merchants, most of whom did not have their own private armies. A fair number of the merchants were Panthay Muslims, who remained quietly in the background despite all the turmoil, trading in opium through proxies. The KKY commanders usually carried their opium to the market town of Tachilek, near the border junction between Burma, Laos, and Thailand. There the opium was exchanged for bars of pure gold—hence the area's nickname, the "Golden Triangle." Opium money was also used to finance the purchase of the consumer goods that the commanders took back as return cargo in their lorries and mule trains. But there is also another explanation to the origin of the name Golden Triangle. It first appeared in print in the *Far Eastern Economic Review* in a July 24, 1971, cover story titled "A Wonderland of Opium." Correspondent T.D. Allman quoted then-United States Assistant Secretary of State Marshall Green as saying that opium was not grown in China and traded by the Chinese communists, as Washington had claimed, but cultivated in a "golden triangle" stretching from northeastern Burma to northern Thailand and northwestern Laos. At the time, Washington was trying to win favor with Beijing. Indeed, in the same month the article appeared it was announced that then-US President Richard Nixon would visit China the following February. The name immediately captured the imagination of the public, as it evoked the lawless nature of opium and its trade. Within a few years, the Golden Triangle—now with capital *G* and *T*—came to symbolize all of Southeast Asia's drug-related problems. The name also caught on in Chinese (*jin sanjiao*) and in Thai (*samliam thongkham*). And although the kind of drugs produced in the Golden Triangle may have changed over the years, we are far from seeing "the tragic end" of the manufacture of narcotics in the area, which Dr. Antonio Maria Costa, executive director of the United Nations Office on Drugs and Crime (UNODC), had claimed in February 2006—or of the devastating influence of the region's drug lords.

The Burmese government was supposed to enforce the law, which officially prohibited drug trafficking. But lacking the power and the political will to do so, government officials were usually content with receiving "tea money" from private merchants and various KKY commanders. Some of the return cargo brought back by the KKY, especially fancy furniture, was given to civilian officials and military officers to lessen their possible opposition to the trade. Government troops sometimes provided security for the KKY's convoys. They also often cooperated with the KKY in the battlefield, in line with the actual purpose of the program. The garrison town of Tang-yan, strategically located between Loi Maw, Loi Sao, Loi Tao, and the other main opium growing areas in northern Shan State, developed into the most important center for the trade.

The KMT acted as a buffer and unofficial border police force for Thailand, and it collected intelligence for Taiwan, the US, and Thailand—in that order. In return the Thai authorities turned a blind eye to the KMT's smuggling activities along the border.

Intelligence agencies from various countries maintained liaison with the KKY, the KMT, and some of the Shan rebel groups, either as pure moneymaking operations or because many of the drug traders proved to be valuable intelligence assets. For historical reasons, Taiwanese agents were especially active, working with not only the remnants of the KMT but also with some of the KKY forces. Since some of these were led by ethnic Chinese from Burma, a relationship was not difficult to establish. The notorious Lo Hsing-han of Kokang KKY was closely connected with Taiwanese intelligence. Taiwan's links with Khun Sa's Loi Maw KKY were maintained through Zhang Suquan, alias Sao Hpalang, a former KMT officer of Manchurian origin who had come to Shan State from Laos in the 1960s. The CIA used as many of the KMT's contacts as possible as their own intelligence assets, and recruited mercenaries to fight another secret war against North Vietnamese troops and local communists in Laos.

International narcotics syndicates inevitably became involved by supplying chemists to the heroin refineries along the Thai-Burmese border, and by taking care of regional and international distribution of the drugs. The syndicates operated independently, but since most of them were dominated by ethnic Chinese often connected with the so-called Secret Societies, or Triads, in Taiwan, Hong Kong, and Macau, links with the KMT and some of the KKY forces were easily established. These crime gangs remain one of the main obstacles to a solution to the conflict in Shan State, since it is in their interest to perpetuate the state of anarchy that makes the drug trade possible. Given the vast amounts of money they possess, their power and influence—as well as their ability to manipulate local rebel leaders, government officials, and drug enforcement agencies—is considerable. Perhaps significantly, international law enforcement agencies seldom turn their attention in the Triads' direction, but tend to concentrate their efforts on the armed bands—and hilltribe peasants—inside Shan State, as if they had contacts in Hong Kong, New York, and Amsterdam.

The couriers were perhaps the most visible links in the narcotics chain, since they were often caught and exposed by the media. A courier could be anyone who was hired by the syndicates to carry drugs from one place to another. The couriers were often conveniently—but incorrectly—referred to by the media as well as law enforcement agencies as drug traffickers—perhaps to deflect attention from the syndicates, which seemed to be above the law. The police usually arrest these couriers, while the big traffickers are seldom caught.

The addicts—the consumers of the drugs—and their families were without doubt the most pitiful victims of the opium business, next to the impoverished farmers who grew the poppies. Although most of the narcotics from the Golden Triangle were destined for foreign markets, it is often forgotten that drug abuse was—and still is—widespread in tribal villages in the Golden Triangle, causing enormous social problems locally. In the 1960s, in some opium growing villages in the Golden Triangle the addiction rate was already as high as 70–80 percent of all male inhabitants.

Occasionally, some drug lords were arrested in Burma, but almost invariably because of links to the rebels, as was the case with Lo Hsing-han in 1973. His rival Khun Sa had been jailed in 1969, reportedly for having opened negotiations with the SSA. But he was released in 1973 after his followers kidnapped two Soviet doctors at the hospital in Taung-gyi. He returned to the Thai border, where he set up base at Ban Hin Taek, northwest of Chiang Rai, and built up a new working relationship with both the Thai and Burmese military authorities. Officially, he now headed not a government-recognized militia unit but a "rebel army" first called the Shan United Army (SUA) and later, when he merged his force with some other private armies, the Möng Tai Army (MTA). However, the absence of any significant fighting for years between the Burmese army and Khun Sa's heavily armed force lent credence to the suggestion that the idea behind the KKY program was not abandoned, just reshaped. To please the Thais, Khun Sa, like the KMT, sent troops in the 1970s to protect road construction crews in insurgent areas. Despite occasional arrests, shifting alliances, and new players in the game, it was business as usual in the Golden Triangle.

But then, in January 1982, Khun Sa was driven out of Ban Hin Taek. His presence on Thai soil had become an international embarrassment and Bangkok decided to act. Heavy fighting raged for days around Ban Hin Taek, until Khun Sa retreated with his men across the border into Burma. He was perhaps down but not out; within months, he had built up a new, sprawling headquarters inside Burma at Homöng opposite Thailand's northwestern Mae Hong Son province. His Möng Tai Army became the biggest and most powerful force in Shan State—and, following the 1989 CPB mutiny, the main rival of the new United Wa State Army (UWSA). Heavy fighting broke out between the two drug armies as the UWSA began to capture territory along the Thai border in the early 1990s.

Through the merger with the non-communist Wa forces on the Thai border, the ex-CPB Was had gained a powerful ally: Wei Xuegang, an ethnic Chinese who had fled with his family into the Wa Hills when the communists came to power in China. At first, Wei and two of his seven brothers and half-brothers, Wei Xuelong and Wei Xueyin, had belonged to the KMT-CIA spy network along the Yunnan frontier, which had an important base at Vingngun north of Panghsang. Vingngun was also the home of Mahasang, the son of Sao Maha, one of the Wa chieftains who had appeared before the 1947 frontier areas committee of enquiry. Mahasang was officially allied with the Burmese government, as he also commanded the local KKY force. But when the CPB took over the Wa Hills, the Wei brothers—and Mahasang—retreated down to the Thai border.

Mahasang ended up as an ally of KMT general Li Wenhuan, while Wei Xuegang joined forces with Khun Sa and became his treasurer. But Wei fell out with Khun Sa, who thought he was being cheated by his wily money-man, and Wei was imprisoned near Ban Hin Taek. He later escaped—some say by bribing his guards—and linked up with his erstwhile Wa allies on the Thai border. When the UWSA was set up, Wei provided it with international connections that the men from Panghsang lacked, as well as business opportunities in Thailand. Wei was once detained briefly in Thailand, but nevertheless managed to continue to maintain contacts with powerful interests in the northern city of Chiang Mai and elsewhere.

Khun Sa was beginning to feel the heat—and in November 1994 Thai authorities, together with the US Drug Enforcement Administration (DEA), launched concerted raids on his organization's known "safe houses" in Thailand. Code-named "Tiger Trap," the operation netted ten of Khun Sa's top lieutenants. The most important of those was Chalee Yangwiri-kul, or Charlie Win. A Sino-Burmese businessman, he was the one who had masterminded the kidnapping of the Soviet doctors in Taunggyi in 1973, and he was later rewarded by Khun Sa with a walled-in residence in Chiang Mai, which also served as a base for his various businesses. Two others nabbed were Na Tsai-kui, an alleged heroin broker who was under indictment by a US court, and Lo Te-ming, Khun Sa's main man in northwest Thailand.

The arrests crippled Khun Sa's supply network in Thailand. Perhaps more important, though, was the seizure of internal MTA documents—including detailed account books—from the safe houses. In one sweep, Khun Sa lost most of his records of who had paid and who owed him money. This led to financial chaos within Khun Sa's organization. A simultaneous blockade by the Burmese Army of the routes from the north, through which opium was convoyed down to his refineries along the

Thai border, further strangled the MTA's economy. His labs, which used to produce exportable heroin, began to crank out methamphetamines, and heroin mixed with methamphetamines.

The pressure on Khun Sa became too strong and, in the first week of January 1996, the old warlord surrendered to the Burmese authorities in a spectacular show at his Homöng headquarters. Government helicopters swept down over the rugged hills to land at Khun Sa's rebel base in the jungle near the Thai border, where thousands of ragtag soldiers were lined up to attention. An entire rebel army had decided not just to lay down their arms, but to hand them over to the government forces in an elaborate ceremony—something which the CPB mutineers never did. Assault rifles, machine guns, rocket launchers, and even SAM-7 surface-to-air missiles were laid out on the ground in front of them as welcoming gifts for the arriving officers from Rangoon.

Khun Sa shook hands with the Burmese officers, and seated beside him was Zhang Shuchuan (alias Sao Hpalang), the powerful Manchurian-born chief of staff of the fifteen-thousand-strong MTA. Khun Sa gave up his base and life as a Golden Triangle warlord and moved to Rangoon with three young Shan girls who had worked in his gem-polishing factory in Homöng. He died in the old Burmese capital on October 27, 2007, spending his last years in a heavily guarded compound. His sons and daughters remained in Shan State, where they became engaged in the local gambling industry as well as the trade in rubies and sapphires. Charlie Win's old house in Chiang Mai was sold to a guest house operator, and few of the tourists who stay there today are aware of what the building once was.

Many other ex-MTA officers also remain in Shan State as local militia commanders, under similar deals with the government as the old KKY in the 1960s and early 1970s—and, gradually, many of them became engaged in the lucrative new drug trade in the Golden Triangle: methamphetamines, or *yaba*, which in the rest of the world are more commonly known as speed pills. What had begun as an emergency solution to the MTA's financial troubles turned into a multi-million dollar business. Wei Xuegang set up a new base at Möng Yawn, across the Thai border from the northern town of Fang, and expertise arrived in the form of a fugitive Thai drug lord, Bang Ron (alias Surachai Ngernthongfoo).

A Sino-Thai drug lord, Bang Ron had run one of Thailand's largest speed distribution networks until the Thai authorities raided his home in Kanchanaburi, west of Bangkok, in October 1998. But he slipped out of the net and managed to escape to Burma over the Three Pagodas Pass, which straddles the border in Kanchanaburi province. Somehow, he then traveled through Burmese government-controlled areas to Wei's base at Möng Yawn, where the duo established new methamphetamine laboratories. Production skyrocketed, and millions of pills poured across the border into Thailand.

Methamphetamine labs were also set up in Panghsang, Möng La, and the other new boom towns near the Chinese border. Officially, the UWSA has its own "Drug Control Task Force"—young men with DCTF embroidered on the insignia on their shoulders—but only two kilometers from the centre of the town is a two-storey wooden building with all windows shuttered. The overpowering and distinctly vanilla-like scent of *yaba* emanates from the structure, in front of which luxury sedans are usually parked amidst flocks of chickens.

According to the Shan Herald Agency for News (SHAN), a Chiang Mai-based Shan media group, foreigners known to be working as chemists in the drug laboratories include Thais as well as Vietnamese. Officially, they are employed at an incense factory, supposedly producing cosmetics for the Chinese market. However, the same herbal oils are also used in the production of *yaba*. They make the drug fragrant and cover up the sometimes harsh odor of the precursor chemicals.

On the road to Pangyang west of Panghsang there is a large, heavily guarded brick building belonging to Wei Xuegang. The smell of strange chemicals can be noticed even from the road, but few travelers would dare to stop to find out exactly what is being produced at this site. Wei's guards tolerate no intruders.

The switch to methamphetamines also coincided with a drop in poppy cultivation in the north. Various UN-sponsored programs, as well as pressure from China to stop the production of heroin, had managed to have some effect on reducing the production of heroin. In the early years of the new century, opium production fell quite substantially in the Wa Hills, and even in Kokang, once Burma's most important opium-producing area. By 2008, Burma's opium production was down to about 450 hundred tons, still significant but not nearly as much as during the opium boom of the 1990s.

It was also a generational shift. The sons and daughters of the old drug lords saw opium and heroin as too messy and a thing of the past. To them, synthetic drugs represented the future. And they were the ones who were going to bring the Golden Triangle up to speed after the decline in poppy cultivation and heroin refining in recent years, spearheading an historic shift in Southeast Asia's production of narcotics. But the basic networks, and many of the players, have remained more or less the same.

FIGURE 36. The Players: 1. Wei Xuegang 2. Wei Xuelong 3. Wei Xueyin 4. Wei Hsaitang 5. Bang Ron 6. Mahasang 7. Mahaja 8. Bao Youliang 9. Bao Youhua 10. Bao Youxiang 11. Sai Leün 12. Xiao Mingliang 13. Bao Youri 14. Yawt Serk 15. Yishe 16. Chao Ngi Lai

FOUR
THE PLAYERS

IT IS a building that one would not have expected to see in the remote and wild mountains of northeastern Burma, close to the Chinese border. But at Nalawt, a small village six kilometers west of the old Burmese communist headquarters of Panghsang, a palatial mansion surrounded by several equally impressive buildings has been erected. Construction under the supervision of an architect from Thailand began in 2006 and the majestic complex was supposed to have been completed in 2007. However, due to additional construction of tunnels, underground living quarters, and bomb-shelters, construction was still going on in 2008 and is expected to be completed by the end of the year. The total cost is estimated at 200 million Chinese renminbi, or nearly US$30 million. A concrete wall surrounds the complex, and on the top of a hill behind the main building are barracks for en elite force of 150 to 200 well-armed soldiers. They are equipped with genuine Russian-made Kalashnikovs, not the Chinese version of the same rifle that is of somewhat inferior quality. Some guards also have US-made M-16 rifles and other automatic weapons.

The owner of the heavily guarded complex is obviously a very rich person—but he may find it difficult to enjoy his wealth. He is wanted by both US and Thai narcotics agencies. The Americans have put a US$2 million bounty on his head, while a Thai court has sentenced him to death in absentia. He is the real merchant of madness: Wei Xuegang, heroin kingpin and overlord of most of the methamphetamine production in the Golden Triangle. And he is the de facto financial controller of the private force that controls the area in which he resides, the United Wa State Army (UWSA).

Little is known about his personal life because—unlike the old drug lord Khun Sa, who liked to bask in publicity—Wei has never given an interview to any foreign journalist or author. There are only two pictures of him in the outside world. One was taken in Thailand in the early 1980s and the other when he was arrested there in November 1988. He had been linked to the seizure of 670 kilograms of heroin and was given a life sentence. But he was released on bail, which had been granted by a Thai judge under mysterious circumstances, and fled across the border to Burma. Higher Thai authorities were furious, and in October 1990 an appeals court overturned the initial verdict and pronounced the death sentence. In July 2001, the Thai interior ministry revoked his Thai citizenship, which he had acquired under the name Prasit Charnchai Chiwinitipanya. He has also been referred to as Somboon Kodumporn.

He had most likely bought somebody else's identity, because his Thai ID card stated that he was born in 1952. In reality, he was born in 1946 in southern Yunnan, somewhere near the Burmese border. His father, Wei Zan, was an opium farmer and a soldier in the nationalist Chinese Kuomintang army. When its remnants withdrew across the border to Burma, Wei's father and the entire family settled in the Vingngun area of the Wa Hills. Wei and his seven-year older brother, Wei Xuelong, and the younger brother, Wei Xueyin, who was born in 1953, grew up in Vingngun, speaking Chinese as well as Wa and Shan. The Wei brothers quickly learned how the KMT and various private armies in the war-torn hills profited from the local opium trade.

In the 1960s their network grew as they established contacts with KMT forces that had settled in northern Thailand. While it is true that the three brothers also maintained connections with the US-backed KMT intelligence network along Burma's border with Yunnan, their main interest was business, not fighting the communists and reconquering China. The flight of Vingngun chieftain Mahasang and the local Ka Kwe Ye home guard forces down to the Thai border following the capture of Vingngun by the Communist Party of Burma (CPB) in 1972 was a blessing in disguise for the Wei brothers. On the Thai border they had even more opportunities to build up their drug empire, especially after ending their erstwhile alliance with Khun Sa and, later, joining forces with the UWSA in 1989.

As the Wei brothers brought their drug trade connections to the UWSA, and allied themselves with fugitive Thai drug lord Bang Ron (also known as Surachai Ngernthongfoo), they also took important roles in the group's financial organization. In 1996 Wei Xuegang, the most powerful of the three brothers, was appointed a member of the central committee of the UWSA's political wing, the United Wa State Party (UWSP), and became commander of the army's 171 Military Region near the Thai border.

The alliance between the "northern," ex-CPB Was and the "southern," non-communist Was enabled the UWSA to spread its influence all the way down to Thailand. Wei was in a unique position to mastermind the merger of the two Wa forces. Although a former KMT-associate, Wei had been doing business with the CPB since the mid-1980s. The Burmese communists controlled the poppy fields, and they sold their opium to Wei, whose refineries along the Thai border turned it into heroin.

The units at the small bases that the old Wa National Council had established on the Thai border after fleeing the Wa Hills in the early 1970s became stronger and better equipped, and, beginning in 1999, tens of thousands of Wa from the north were relocated to the south. Entire new towns were established just across the border from Thailand, and the original inhabitants of the area, mostly ethnic Shans, were driven out. Wei established a southern headquarters near Möng Yawn, a former stronghold of Khun Sa's Möng Tai Army (MTA). But, as Khun Sa had surrendered to Burma's military authorities in January 1996, old MTA areas were taken over by the UWSA, and a stream of Shan refugees into Thailand followed.

The war with the UWSA had greatly contributed to the demise of the MTA, and, as an incentive, the Burmese government had granted the Was the right to take over all territories adjacent to the Thai border formerly controlled by Khun Sa's men. Thus, the UWSA gained increased access to strategically important border areas, through which Wei and his associates could conduct their trade in various kinds of contraband. An entirely new, even larger Wa base area sprung up in the south, a territory which had never before been populated by Was.

According to Colonel Kyaw Thein, a leading member of Burma's antidrug committee, the relocation was "part of efforts to eradicate opium, from which heroin is made." The plan, he and his UWSA allies said, was to move Was from the opium growing areas in the north to the fertile valleys of southern Shan State, where they could grow other crops.

Not everyone was convinced that was the main objective, however. By gaining control of this strategic border area, the UWSA could buy supplies from Thailand—and send drugs across. Wei and other UWSA leaders made huge profits due to direct access to the Thai market and enabled them to expand their army as well as the territory under its control.

In June 2000, a Thai military spokesman told the British Broadcasting Corporation (BBC) that the relocation had led to about fifty new meth-amphetamine laboratories springing up along the border. He believed each of those laboratories could produce up to one hundred thousand *yaba* pills per day, more than three times the production rate before the relocations were made. In the year after the relocation, more than forty million *yaba* pills were seized in Thailand, most of which were made in the new Wa base area across the northern border.

Wei thus took the helm of the strategic shift from exclusive reliance on opium and its derivative heroin to industrial scale production of meth-amphetamines. Moreover, he masterminded the swift mass proliferation of synthetic narcotics across mainland Southeast Asia. The financial crisis that swept the region in 1997 also played a role in the success of the shift. Many drug users could no longer afford heroin, and *yaba* became a cheaper alternative. For some reason, many young people thought that *yaba* was less addictive and not as dangerous as heroin.

In 2002, as his residence in Nalawt was on the drawing board, Wei turned over day-to-day command of the 171 Military Region to his younger brother, Xueying. But he remained the effective commander of the force, directing it by remote control from Nalawt, and sometimes from the Bur-mese garrison town of Tang-yan, where he also had a base. And he has indeed been nicknamed by his associates the "remote control"; in a career in narcotics spanning four decades Wei Xuegang has bankrolled various militias, all while demonstrating an aptitude for knowing when to make and break alliances.

He can also be exceedingly brutal. On January 7, 1998, the Wa pointman in Thailand, Sai Pao, or Ai Pao-sin, was gunned down outside a luxury hotel in Chiang Mai as he was on his way to attend the wedding of Wa chieftain Mahasang's daughter. His assailant was riding a motorbike and wearing a police uniform. According to Thai intelligence sources, Wei had contacted corrupt elements within the police in northern Thailand, who hired a gunman to kill Sai Pao. Wei was frustrated with Sai Pao, who had undercut his price by one or two baht per pill. Prior to that, the two men had worked together.

The younger brother, Wei Xueyin, is not of the same caliber, and is said to be rather clumsy. In June 2007, he even managed to shoot himself in the leg while getting out of a vehicle somewhere in southern Shan State. The firearm was tucked in the front of his trousers. The elder brother, Wei Xuelong, was involved in UWSA affairs in the years after the formation of the organization, but has since faded away. He is said to be in poor health, suffering from chronic kidney disease.

On July 4, 2006—by coincidence or not, US Independence Day—Wei Xuegang was appointed by the UWSP's politburo as financial affairs chief, a post which he held until late December 2007, when he was succeeded by his former deputy, Bao Youliang, younger brother of the UWSP/UWSA supremo, Bao Youxiang. While Bao Youliang is considered by UWSA insiders to be largely inexperienced for the position, there is ample evidence to suggest the move to remove Wei was largely cosmetic, as the organization was embarrassed by Wei's presence in an official position. Youliang's main official business in his own name is a company that exports oolong

FIGURE 37. Wei's Mansion at Nalawt

tea to Taiwan. The packaging has a picture of him in the corner, wearing a farmer's hat.

In other words, Wei Xuegang remains the bankroller of the organization, although he does not hold an official title within the organization. In his role as the "remote control," furthermore, Wei also gives the UWSA the opportunity to deny that they are actively involved in the drugs business, as they can conveniently point a finger at the wily Wei and continue to claim that they are not involved at any level in the Golden Triangle drug trade. It is a weak argument, however, accepted only by a handful of naive reporters on the matter.

Wei probably also does not want to hold any official, and therefore potentially exposed, office. He is known to be highly paranoid and avoids public gatherings for fear of cameras. "Politics are for fools," he once said. People close to him say that he cooks his own food because he is afraid of being poisoned. When he ventures outside his residence he is always guarded by at least one hundred men from his private security force. He changes vehicles several times per trip, as he believes he is followed by US reconnaissance drones.

Most of the time, however, Wei is said to remain inside his magnificent castle in the mountains. He is not known to drink, smoke, use drugs, or womanize, preferring to spend his nights reading books or watching TV and DVD movies. He rarely goes to sleep before daybreak. He hates the sun and wears a camouflage fatigue jacket zipped up to his neck, which people who have seen him say covers a bulletproof vest. Not a happy life for a multi-billionaire.

THE BAO BROTHERS AND THEIR ASSOCIATES

Although they grew up in the Wa Hills, the Wei brothers are ethnic Chinese and could not, therefore, qualify as leaders of the Wa. Like the CPB before them, they needed to operate through local Wa chieftains, and a mutually beneficial relationship developed between the Wei and the Bao brothers. But it has not always been smooth, as the Baos, unlike the Weis, do not think that "politics is for fools." The Baos may have grown rich on the drug trade as well, but they have also shown some concern for the civilian population in the area.

The first UWSP leader, Chao Ngi Lai, was perhaps the most political of the Wa chieftains. A veteran guerrilla fighter, he was known to be calm under fire and a shrewd, rational decision maker. He came from a poor family, and his parents gave him away as a child to a Wa leader in Saohin (Pangwei) who was also a Christian. Not more than 10 percent of the Wa are Christian, but their influence in the northern Wa Hills was significant before the area was taken over by the CPB in the late 1960s and early 1970s. After the 1989 mutiny, Chao Ngi Lai converted to Christianity to honor his late adoptive father. The break with his CPB past was complete.

But following Chao Ngi Lai's stroke in 1995 the Baos—to whom politics and business were intertwined—took over and developed a commercial empire of their own. The Asian edition of *Time*, in a cover story on the Was on December 16, 2002, estimated that the UWSA's business interests earned its elite commanders and their associates up to US$550 million a year.

Much has changed since the days that Bao Youxiang led his Wa troops, under CPB command, through the jungles of Shan State. He was the Wa officer who had a bowling alley built in Panghsang with a lane reserved for himself, which may contradict the assumption that he has the good of his Wa people at heart. Surely, poor Wa farmers must have more important needs than a bowling alley, and the money could have been spent more wisely on a school or rural clinic. He is also rumored to have killed a masseuse in China because he was not happy with her service. On another occasion, in the late 1990s, he reportedly ordered and watched four of his associates pistol-whipped to death because he thought they were conspiring against him.

Like Wei, Bao has been affected by the same affliction that many drug lords suffer from: paranoia. He suffers from an acute and chronic case of incurable trichinosis, which he got from eating uncooked pork when he was with the CPB. Called *neu som* in Shan, and *naem* in Thai, it is a pickled kind of pork that is safe to eat if prepared properly, which is not always the case. To mitigate the effects of the disease he has consulted the same traditional Chinese medical practitioner for years. But even so, Bao always orders him to prepare twice the normally prescribed amount of herbal potion. Bao first watches him prepare it, then insists that the man consume one-half himself. Only then will Bao take his dose. Bao, like Wei, is afraid of being poisoned.

The trichinosis appears to have affected Bao's brain. Four associates who met him in 2008 had to speak with him individually and without interruption as both his attention span and memory had become noticeably weak. "If he is interrupted, he forgets everything he has just heard," one of the associates said. But he has nevertheless been able to lead the UWSP and the UWSA. And he has managed to control much of the drug trade in his area, making himself and his brothers rich in the process.

There were four Bao brothers when Panghsang and other towns in the Wa Hills were transformed from ramshackle CPB-run clusters of bamboo-huts into modern towns. The eldest, Bao Youri, now drives a Hummer model H2-2007 that, for reasons no one can explain, sports California number plates. The only other known Hummer in Burma is owned by Tay Za, an immensely wealthy tycoon who lives in Rangoon and is closely connected with General Than Shwe, the leader of the ruling State Peace and Development Council (SPDC.) Bao Youri oversees the drug business in southern Shan State and is perhaps closer to Wei Xuegang than to his younger brother, Youxiang.

Brother number three, Bao Youliang, is the unofficial governor of Möng Mao in the northern Wa Hills. He is also close to Wei, first as his deputy in financial affairs and then, supposedly, as his boss. But no one doubts that it is Wei who still controls the coffers. None of the ethnic Wa leaders has his business acumen and contacts in the region and beyond.

The youngest brother, Bao Youhua, on the other hand, was always close to Bao Youxiang. And he was even more ruthless than his brother. He had an estate near the airport in the border town of Tachilek, opposite Mae Sai in Thailand, with a fishpond, drug storage sheds—and a detention facility with a torture chamber. People who had defaulted on their drug debts to him, or those he thought had tried to double-cross him, ended up there. Youhua, reportedly, took an active part in the torture of the wretched men.

Bao Youhua was also a heavy drinker and womanizer, and the only one of the four brothers who liked the drug they produced. He consumed vast quantities of *yaba*, and eventually died from a massive stroke on August 26, 2007. He was buried at a grand ceremony at Hkwin Ma, the Baos' home village in the northern Wa Hills. He was only forty-eight and is survived by seventeen children. It is not known how many wives he had.

But the Baos—and the Weis—never worked alone. Bao Youxiang's son-in-law, an ethnic Wa from China called Ho Chung, handles money-laundering operations for the Baos and the Weis. He is also a frequent visitor to the annual gems auction in Rangoon and is considered close to Burmese military intelligence agents, with whom he plays golf. He is married to the second of Bao's four daughters, Bao Yina, a formidable businesswoman in her own right.

Xiao Minliang, also a younger man, serves as vice-chairman of the UWSP and is the main spokesman for the organization. He often meets representatives from the United Nations Office on Drugs and Crime (UNODC), and even foreign journalists and researchers. He is quoted extensively in *The United Wa State Party: Narco-Army or Ethnic Nationalist Party?* by Dutch drug researcher Tom Kramer. The weakness of that study is that the author tends to take at face value what is said by the UWSP's leaders and the Burmese military's drug czar, Colonel Hkam Awng.

Xiao Minliang is quoted as admitting that there were heroin refineries and methamphetamine laboratories under their control "up to 1998," but "after that we banned all heroin and [methamphetamine] refineries in our area." But then Kramer states that in September 2005, seven years after the "ban," Burmese authorities confiscated nearly five hundred kilograms of heroin that was coming out of the UWSP's territory. This was unusual, but sources on the ground assert that the right officers had not been paid off, so the bust was made.

Xiao Minliang, in fact, is Wei Xuegang's spokesman—and his eyes and ears when foreign visitors come to Panghsang. He is also known to have acted as a go-between for Wei in negotiations with Burma's military rulers. UWSA insiders say that Xiao is, in fact, Wei's figurehead in the organization. Unlike Wei, Xiao is an ethnic Wa and could well become Bao Youxiang's successor, if his health continues to deteriorate. According to some sources, Wei's mother may have been Wa, but he is culturally and in all other respects Chinese.

However, despite potential business conflicts and personal ambitions, the UWSP/UWSA leadership has managed to maintain a remarkable unity. The only serious conflict erupted when Wei Hsaitang, who is also known as Ta Htang, was arrested in 2002. No relation to the Wei brothers, he was a field commander popular with the UWSA rank and file. He led several battles against rival gangs and armies along the Thai border, especially Khun Sa's MTA.

But Wei Xuegang considered him an archenemy because of his strong position in the southern border areas. Ta Htang was accused of counterfeiting Chinese and Burmese banknotes, but the charge was most probably just an excuse for having him arrested, even though Wei produced the "evidence" that resulted in his conviction. Ta Htang, for his part, felt that he had not got his fair share of the new business empire that Wei had built up on the Thai border. Ta Htang had done the fighting while Wei had reaped the profits and, at the same time, lined his own pockets. Ta Htang made some money from the *yaba* trade, but not nearly as much as Wei. At one stage he ordered Wei to leave his new base at Möng Yawn—or pay one hundred thousand baht for each of the many UWSA soldiers who had died under his command while taking over Khun Sa's territory.

However, Ta Htang ended up spending only five years of his fifty-year sentence in a jail in Panghsang. He was released in May 2007 and called back to the UWSA military headquarters. Bao Youxiang considered him one of the UWSA's best field commanders, and his qualities were needed to discipline younger soldiers who, after the end of the bloody war against the MTA, had no combat experience other than occasional clashes with Thai border guards and rival militias in southern Shan State. Bao also suggested that the two archrivals should reconcile, but Wei declined.

The arrest and relatively swift rehabilitation of Ta Htang could reflect a deep conflict of interest between Wei Xuegang and Bao Youxiang. Some sources have suggested that Bao is concerned that Wei might consolidate power within the organization and then reach a deal with the ruling junta involving the disarmament of the UWSA in exchange for assurances of a comfortable retirement for himself in Rangoon—as Khun Sa achieved with his MTA. Ta Htang is believed to be loyal to Bao but was nevertheless not allowed to stay long at Panghsang. In March 2008 he was moved to

Nam Teuk, the northernmost town in the UWSA-controlled area. Located on the banks of the Nam Ting river and close to the Chinese border, it has become a boom town, rivaling even Lin Mingxian's Möng La. The man in charge of Nam Teuk is one of Bao's most trusted nephews.

Ta Htang's move to Nam Teuk was an effort by Bao to minimize the risk of a broader split within the organization. At the time of Ta Htang's release there were speculations that if either he or Wei was assassinated it could lead to widespread infighting, as their respective support bases would be brought into the fray, a scenario that Bao was intent on avoiding. Clearly, Panghsang was not big enough for both Ta Htang and Wei. At the same time, Bao had a definite interest in cultivating Ta Htang for future contingencies, should a power struggle break out within the UWSA. After all, Ta Htang is a Wa while Wei is not. There is always the risk that Wei might sell out to the Burmese government and reach a deal similar to that achieved by Khun Sa in 1996. Both Bao and Ta Htang are no doubt also in the drug trade, but they also have other, national interests at heart.

For the time being, however, no serious conflict is likely to erupt between Wei and Bao. They need each other. Without the Baos' physical control over a large territory, Wei would never under present circumstances be able to conduct his nefarious businesses in peace. And without Wei, the Baos would not have access to the regional and international crime networks through which they market illicit products from their area. And this is precisely one of the critical points that UNODC officials, as well as certain researchers who have written on the subject, seem to have thus far overlooked or otherwise chosen to ignore.

THE RED GUARDS

On November 2, 1993, armed guards dragged three frightened men out into the central marketplace of Möng La. Hands tied behind their backs, the men were ashen with fear. The entire population of Möng La had been ordered to attend the spectacle. The three wretched men were lined up in front of a firing squad of young soldiers, some of them barely in their teens. They raised their Chinese-made Kalashnikovs and opened fire.

The crowd looked on as the three prisoners were cut down by a hail of bullets. Their bloodied bodies were left in the marketplace as a deterrent. A few days before, it had been discovered that the trio were involved in an attempt to assassinate Lin Mingxian, the former Red Guard volunteer who had become the overlord of one of the busiest boom towns on the Sino-Burmese border.

He is also typical of the new chieftains in the Golden Triangle, who don't have to hide in the jungle like Khun Sa and other drug lords of the 1970s and 1980s. Thanks to the 1989 cease-fire agreements between the forces of the former CPB and the Burmese government, Lin is instead enjoying all the benefits of public life. In the 1990s he even attended a National Convention in Rangoon that was aimed at drafting a new constitution for Burma. Eventually, in May 2008—when a cyclone had devastated almost the entire delta of the Irrawaddy River and the country was facing a severe humanitarian crisis—a referendum was held, and, if official figures are to be believed, more than 90 percent voted in favor of the new charter.

In August 1993—three months before the public execution at his Möng La stronghold—Lin even played host to an unofficial delegation of US politicians, which included Congressman Charles Rangel, erstwhile chairman of the now dissolved House Committee on Narcotics. Rangel had for years been friendly with the Burmese generals and, on one occasion, said in an interview with the US television network CBS: "They're saying that the Burmese army is brutal. Hey! Of course they have to be brutal; they're fighting a war on drugs."

And in December, barely a month after the ghastly spectacle in Möng La, an even more incongruous group of visitors passed by Lin's hilltop residence near the Yunnan frontier: a car rally organized by the Tourist Authority of Thailand. A convoy of forty-six jeeps and other four-wheel-drive vehicles, with stickers advertising motor oil and travel agencies, sped through the area on their way from northern Thailand to Kunming in Yunnan. It was the first rally of its kind and the stated purpose was to promote friendship between the peoples of Thailand, Burma, Laos, and China.

Lin's rise to prominence followed a pattern unlike that of any other kingpin in the Golden Triangle. He was born around 1950 in the town of Panghsai, of mixed Shan-Chinese parentage. Panghsai is marked as "Kyu

Hkok" on most maps and it is here that the fabled Burma Road crosses the international frontier into Yunnan. At that time an old Bailey bridge spanned the Nam Yan border stream and connected Panghsai with its sister town, Wanting, in China. During World War II, tons of vital war supplies were trucked across that bridge and on to frontline positions in southern China, where KMT forces were resisting the Japanese advance.

By the time Lin was born, this traffic had long ceased. He was a child when thousands of KMT soldiers came streaming in the other direction, away from Mao Zedong's victorious communists and into northeastern Burma. And the Panghsai area was spared from the KMT's terror, which also cost the life of Lin's own mother in 1967. Lin, then in his teens, walked across the bridge into Wanting and joined the Red Guards. The Cultural Revolution was sweeping across China and millions of young people were inspired by Chairman Mao's militant message. The young Lin teamed up with an old childhood friend in Wanting, Zhang Zhiming. Born in the year after the communist victory in China, Zhang was a true son of the revolution. His parents had given him the name "Zhiming," which means "bright ideals." Another comrade was the slightly older Li Ziru from Baoshan, a town some 280 kilometers northwest of Wanting.

It was hardly surprising that the young idealists Lin, Zhang, and Li were among the thousands of Red Guards who streamed across the border to fight alongside their Burmese comrades in the CPB. They lived close to Burma, and they were young and wanted to see action. At the battle-front, Lin fell in love with an ethnic Chinese girl from Rangoon, Than Than Win. She had fled to China when anti-Chinese riots struck Rangoon in 1967, the pretext Beijing needed to support the CPB more openly. Than Than Win, who had been working in a factory in Kunming, had also volunteered to go back and fight.

"She was young and pretty, and the couple spent hours together, reading quotations from Mao's little red book," an old friend of Lin and Than Than Win recalls. "They were full of revolutionary fervor and believed in a red future for Burma." Lin and Than Than Win were married in 1973 at a simple ceremony organized by the party.

When nearly all of the Chinese "volunteers" were called back to China after the death of Mao in 1976, Lin, Zhang, and Li were left behind, most probably because of their familiarity with the area and their knowledge of local languages, which they had acquired as young men in the hills of northeastern Burma. More specifically, they were expected to collect valuable intelligence information for the Public Security Bureau in Yunnan, China's equivalent of the FBI, the CIA, the KGB, and the local traffic police all rolled into one.

The three Chinese "volunteers" were positioned strategically in different parts of the twenty thousand square kilometer territory controlled by the Burmese communists along the frontier with Yunnan. Zhang became commander of the northern forces, and Li was based at the communist headquarters at Panghsang. Lin was appointed commander of the CPB's base area in the easternmost corner of Burma, bordering both China and Laos.

Lin had led several campaigns against government forces in the hills north of Kengtung when Than Than Win contracted blackwater fever. Officially, China's support to the Burmese communists had ceased, but in reality they still had access to Yunnan for supplies and medical treatment. Than Than Win died in 1980 in a hospital in Lancang in Yunnan.

Lin was grief-stricken, old comrades say, but he soon recovered. Only a few months after Than Than Win's death, he married another Chinese girl, this time a young woman from Kokang, an area inside Burma under communist control and dominated by ethnic Yunnanese. She was plump and unattractive—but her father, Peng Jiasheng, the chieftain of Kokang, was in the opium business and therefore rich by local standards.

After the 1989 mutiny, Peng began sending large quantities of heroin from his refineries into China. Son-in-law Lin, who together with his old comrade-in-arms and fellow ex-Red Guard Zhang Zhiming (who had come down to Möng La after the mutiny) was in control of the easternmost part of the former communist area, linked up with ethnic Chinese crime syndicates in Southeast Asia and looked east. A new heroin route was opened through Laos and down to the island of Koh Kong off the coast of Cambodia. Anti-narcotics officials have also detected another route via Laos to the port of Danang in Vietnam.

The choice of Laos as a transit country is no coincidence. In the 1970s anti-Vietnamese rebels were operating in Laos, and they could not cross that country's border into China for training because of the very large Vietnamese presence there. They had to detour through easternmost Burma, and Lin's men escorted them through their territory to secret training camps in Yunnan. Thus, Lin had contacts in Laos, but the first attempts to use his old friends in the resistance failed; they were disorganized and powerless. And China's interest in supporting anti-government rebels in Laos faded as new, more businesslike foreign policy priorities were adopted.

Lin then made a bold move: he contacted corrupt elements in the Lao military, who needed little persuasion to cooperate. Furthermore, it was not difficult to take advantage of the chaos that existed in war-torn Cambodia. Before long, Koh Kong became one of the largest transshipment points for narcotics leaving Southeast Asia. Lin was able to capitalize on his various connections in Laos, which later enabled him to expand his businesses in that country.

In the beginning, business in Lin's area was monopolized by a committee of thirteen persons, including, of course, Lin himself and his companion Zhang. They decided how the raw opium should be collected and where the refineries should be established. All produce is sold centrally, and the various "shareholders" in the "company" drew dividends from the profits. Money was then reinvested in real estate in Rangoon and Mandalay, Yunnan, northern Thailand, and even Hong Kong and Taiwan.

Thanks to the 1989 cease-fire agreement with the Burmese government, Lin's contacts soon included high-ranking officers in the army and the powerful intelligence apparatus, as well as government ministers. Even the official Burmese newspaper the *Working People's Daily* (now renamed the *New Light of Myanmar*), carried pictures of Lin shaking hands with junta leaders in Rangoon; his name, though, has been Burmanized to "U Sai Lin."

In May 1991, Lin even invited diplomats and UN officials from Rangoon to attend a "drug-burning ceremony" at his Möng La headquarters. Needless to say, it did not impress many. But nobody protested, either. A front-page picture in the *Working People's Daily* showed a smiling Lin sitting side by side with members of the ruling junta, foreign defense attachés from Rangoon, and the then Chinese ambassador to Burma, Chang Ruisheng.

Lin's contacts in China, which go back to the old days, have always been excellent. It is widely suspected that neither Lin nor Zhang—nor Li Ziru, the third ex-Red Guard who remained behind in northeastern . Burma—ever gave up their contacts with the Public Security Bureau in Yunnan. This may explain why Lin has been able to own a fortified mansion in Jinghong in southern Yunnan. He also runs a hotel in the same town, a cigarette factory at his headquarters at Möng La, and trading companies in Burma as well as Yunnan. As a result, the town of Daluo, directly across the border from Möng La, has also experienced rapid economic growth. It is not as prosperous as Möng La, but much richer than it was during the CPB era.

But the Chinese were not pleased to see vast amounts of money disappearing into the casinos, strip joints, and transvestite shows that the former Red Guard had set up in Möng La. In the early 2000s, an estimated three thousand Chinese tourists crossed the border every day, and they were big spenders—-and losers. Billions of yuan renminbi, Chinese currency, were siphoned off from government coffers by corrupt officials and squandered at baccarat tables in Möng La. After repeated threats leveled by Beijing fell on Lin's stubborn ears, in January 2005 Chinese security forces breached the border, stormed casinos, and rounded up Chinese gamblers. A few gaming halls were damaged and the border crossing was effectively sealed. The once bustling Möng La turned into a ghost town.

However, the border was eventually reopened, and in late April 2006 Lin presided over the inauguration of a new set of seven, out of a total of twenty-one, casinos that were being built, all located at Möng Ma, sixteen kilometers from the border. The business has grown since then, and there are now no less than fifty-two gaming houses at Wan Hsieo, a small village near Möng Ma town whose main features only a few years before were rickety bamboo huts, some paddy fields, and a few wandering water buffaloes.

This string of casinos has a new high-tech feature that allows Chinese gamblers to place bets online from the convenience of their homes—which effectively makes it possible to circumvent Chinese government efforts to prevent an outbound flow of cash. Suspended from the ceilings in Möng Ma are cameras connected to high-speed internet, so gamblers can watch the gaming tables and, by mobile phone, communicate with agents on location at the jungle casinos. The agents place bets on behalf of the gamblers, who then transfer funds into the casino operators' China-based bank accounts. Online players bet up to four or five million renminbi, or approximately US$143,000–286,000. A specific casino visited by one of the authors was said to be able to handle bets up to US$1 million daily in June 2006. In the center of the hall of the main casino sits a giant Buddha statue, which placidly overlooks the entire operation.

Lin also began to build another gaming town at the confluence of the Nam Lwe and Mekong rivers. Called Sop Lwe—"the mouth of the Lwe" in Shan—it also became known as "911" after Lin's military units in the area: the former ninth and eleventh brigades of the CPB's army. His National Democratic Alliance Army (Eastern Shan State) fields about three thousand soldiers, most of whom are Akha and Shan conscripts. Several of its units have been deployed to handle the transport of various kinds of contraband from Sop Lwe across the river into Laos, or downriver to Thailand and beyond.

In 1997 Lin had in fact declared his area "drug-free," and all trade in narcotics was said to have ceased. It was to commemorate that event that he built a museum dedicated to the end of poppy cultivation in the Möng La area, complete with pictures of him receiving Burmese and foreign dignitaries. But Thai and Western narcotics officials have their doubts. There may not be many opium poppies left in his area, but *yaba* is available to anyone who wants to buy it.

Today, Lin, the old Red Guard, lives in a palatial Miami Beach-style pink mansion perched above Möng La, resembling the residence of a feudal warlord raised above his jungle fiefdom. And all has been built on the proceeds of the drug trade. On his front lawn he has his initials "SL," for Sai Leün, carved into the well-groomed hedges that adorn his fortress.

Lin's younger brother, Sai Toon, commands two of his brigades and is responsible for the strategically important tri-border area of Burma, China, and Laos. Sai Toon is linked to one of the UWSA's *yaba* factories in Panghsang and oversees shipments on the Mekong river. A March 2008 document from Thailand's Office of Narcotics Control Board describes the relationship between Bao Youxiang and Lin: "The latter is involved in narcotics trade including production, distribution, and precursors to support production factories." According to the same document, Bao Ching, a relative of Bao Youxiang, is vice president of Lin's NDAA (ESS) and coordinator of logistics for drug movements from the northern Wa Hills through Möng La to Sop Lwe and down the river to Thailand.

Möng La's strategic position and its proximity to land as well as river routes down to Thailand and eastward to Laos gives Lin a strong, central position in the contraband trade. And his connections in China are unique. Essentially, born of former Red Guard associations, the relationship between the UWSA and the NDAA (ESS) is vitally important to both groups, strategically as well as economically. Significantly, the UWSA maintains an office in Möng La, and in 2007 there were four UWSA battalions stationed in Lin's area, underscoring the close relationship between the two ex-CPB armies.

Lin is further linked to Chinese Muslim, Panthay (or Chin Haw), and ethnic Lahu networks based at Lao Khai in Kokang, where his father-in-law is also still active in the trade. According to intelligence sources, those networks now operate a laboratory in Lao Khai where chemists are producing an imitation of ecstasy called *ya-ee* (the "*ee*" is for "ecstasy"). It is not real MDMA, methylenedioxymethamphetamine or ecstasy, but a high-grade type of speed, and the main markets for the drug are said to be in Hong Kong and Malaysia.

Lin has suffered two strokes, the second of which left him paralyzed for months. But he appears to have recovered and is often seen in Möng La and around the casinos in Möng Ma. His old comrade Li Ziru, however, was less fortunate. He died on January 5, 2005, after having served as deputy commander-in-chief and chief-of-staff of the UWSA since the mutiny in 1989. Li Ziru was the first prominent warlord to set up base at Nalawt, and it is widely believed that he was in the drug business even before the collapse of the CPB. Li's part of the business in Panghsang is now run by his son, Li Zuhua, and nephew, Li Ching. They still live in Panghsang and have residences in Menglian, across the border in China. In Menglian they manage the Ru Yi ("Anything You Want") Hotel and the attached "Wa Street" entertainment complex, which boasts duty-free shops and karaoke bars with "hostesses." There is also a nightclub where dancers gyrate under strobe lights in a cloud of smoke—and with a fine white powder falling from the ceiling, which to some visitors would serve as a reminder of what kind of trade provided the proceeds that built this complex.

Zhang Zhiming, however, keeps a very low profile, even though he was instrumental in transforming Möng La into a booming gambling center. This could be because of the fact that he has retained his citizenship of the People's Republic of China and is still in active service for various agencies in his real homeland.

Who is Yawt Serk?

Khun Sa's surrender in January 1996 sent shockwaves through Shan State and Shan communities in Thailand. His MTA was not only a drug trafficking organization. Many Shan nationalists flocked to Khun Sa because he had power and money, and they were not the slightest bit interested in his Golden Triangle drug trade. But there were also others, mostly ethnic Chinese, for whom the trade in narcotics was more important than preserving Shan culture—not unlike the situation in the UWSA today, where men like Wei Xuegang pursue their drug business with no interest in politics while the Bao brothers and some other Wa leaders may also harbor nationalist sentiments. The title of Kramer's book *The United Wa State Army: Narco-Army or Ethnic Nationalist Party?* is, therefore, misleading. It is possible to be both.

But not everyone in the MTA agreed to lay down their arms. A group led by a young Shan commander called Yawt Serk went up into the hills, where they resurrected the Shan United Revolutionary Army (SURA), the group that the late Moh Heing had founded when he broke away from the Shan State Army (SSA) in 1969.

The choice of the name was no coincidence. Yawt Serk, who was born in Möng Nawng near Kehsi Mansam in 1959, had joined the SURA at the age of seventeen. He had little formal education, only up to middle school in the central Shan State town of Panglong, but he was bright and became a radio operator in Moh Heing's army. When Moh Heing joined forces with Khun Sa in March 1985, Yawt Serk became a low-ranking commander in the larger force, which in 1987 assumed the name MTA. And the new commander's name had also been carefully chosen: "Yawt Serk" is Shan for "best at war."

In 1998, two years after Khun Sa's surrender, Yawt Serk's reconstituted SURA was renamed SSA, though sometimes with "South" added to the name to distinguish it from the "old" SSA in northern Shan State, which in 1989 entered into a cease-fire agreement with the Burmese government. Yawt Serk's SSA built up a string of bases along the Thai border—and almost immediately clashed with the UWSA as the Was were expanding their influence south.

Yawt Serk's relationship with the Thai authorities has always been a matter of conjecture. He was undoubtedly able to procure equipment for his troops from the Thai side, and many young Shans who had been arrested for illegal entry in Thailand were released if they agreed to join his army. The Thais evidently wanted someone to keep an eye on developments across the border in Burma, beyond their reach, and, especially, to monitor the establishment of *yaba* laboratories on the other side. The laboratories also had to be destroyed, and sometimes Yawt Serk's SSA could be called upon to carry out such tasks.

But he did not become a fully trusted ally of the Thais. Thai military intelligence sources argue that on various occasions the SSA hit-teams on the ground would return to the border claiming that certain laboratories had been eliminated. The Thais would later learn that this had not always been the case. It also became clear that Yawt Serk taxed *yaba* consignments passing through his territory. An army major in Thailand once complained about Yawt Serk: "He is clean in front. But we must always check his back."

Some defenders of Yawt Serk maintain that he is not in any way involved in the drug trade, although some of his men may buy and sell *yaba*. Others say that he is only taxing the trade, not taking an active part in it. A source close to Yawt Serk asserted that this is not an entirely correct picture: "He knows exactly what goes on and who in his organization is involved. He himself is aware of all deals and arrangements that are made." And his involvement is not limited to "taxation," the source said: "First of all, they do not call it taxation. Instead they refer to it as 'contributions' to the Shan cause. They will deal with other trafficking groups and say 'we know what you're up to. We know what you're doing. Perhaps you should contribute to the cause.'" That can be done either in cash or, at times, in weaponry. Yawt Serk's SSA would then turn a blind eye to the traffickers' movements in exchange for some automatic rifles. The same source said of Yawt Serk's alleged involvement in the drug trade: "What else can he do? He has no choice but to be involved."

But Yawt Serk and his men have also attacked and destroyed *yaba* laboratories, which has earned him some praise from the Thai side. They have also destroyed drugs seized at those laboratories and invited foreign journalists to witness the bonfires. And he has managed to gain the sympathy of many Thais for his cause—independence from Burma. Among the celebrities who have made it to his main camp at Loi Taileng, opposite Thailand's Mae Hong Son province, is the famous Thai folk singer Ad Carabao, who even composed some songs to honor the Shans. The album, *Mai Dtong Ronghai*, or "Don't Cry," combines reggae rhythms with strong lyrics expressing support for the Shan struggle for freedom. Thai monthly magazines have written extensively about Yawt Serk and published photo essays featuring his troops. The Thais and the Shans are, after all, ethnic cousins.

Other ex-MTA commanders have preferred to maintain a working relationship with the Burmese army. Among them is Mahaja, the younger half-brother of Wa chieftain Mahasang—although Mahasang, like Yawt Serk, had established links to forces on the Thai side of the border. He was arrested in March 2005 during a drug-sting operation that went wrong, and died in hospital in Chiang Mai in December 2007. Mahaja, though, continued to roam the mountains north of Khun Sa's old headquarters in Homöng together with a force of ex-MTA soldiers. And he is a heavy *yaba* user. He even took pills when he was attending the National Convention in Rangoon in the early 2000s.

Naw Kham, an Shan and also a former MTA officer, became a local military leader and a prominent drug trafficker after Khun Sa's surrender. He based himself at Tachilek and began to operate along the Mekong river. Naw Kham not only trades in *yaba* but smokes it as well. An associate of his says that he can smoke a whopping forty pills in just two hours, five at a time, and go through three lighters in the process.

Naw Kham earned notoriety when, on February 25, 2008, his men ambushed a Chinese government patrol boat on the Mekong about thirty kilometers north of the Thai river port of Chiang Saen. Several Chinese crewmembers were shot and others repeatedly stabbed. No one died in the attack, but several Chinese were severely injured and had to receive treatment at a hospital in Chiang Rai.

There were varying rumors as to the motive for the assault, which took place just before dawn. According to one source, Naw Kham sought revenge after he had found out that the patrol boat had been running *yaba* shipments for another player who had undercut his own fees for transporting drugs on the river. Another rumor has it that the patrol boat was carrying cash originating in Möng La and picked up at Lin Mingxian's port of Sop Lwe. The money was then going to be transported to the site of two new mega casino complexes that Lin is building with some Chinese investors near Ban Huay Xay in Laos, across the river from the Thai town of Chiang Khong. It is likely that the real motive for the night-time strike was essentially robbery, but it is unclear how much the attackers managed to get from the patrol boat.

Naw Kham is one of few drug lords in the area who has homes in all three Golden Triangle countries. Apart from the one in Tachilek, he also owns a house on the eastern bank of the Mekong river near Möng Mom in Laos's Bo Keo province, and another on the outskirts of Chiang Saen in Thailand, where the Nam Ruak joins the Mekong.

According to several local sources, Naw Kham is being protected by the Burmese army commander in the Tachilek area. Following pressure from China, Burmese authorities raided Naw Kham's house in Tachilek in 2006—but he was tipped off by the local commander and escaped. The raid reportedly netted 140 assorted weapons, two compressors for making *yaba*, and millions of speed pills. The weaponry that was seized included one m-60mm mortar, one surface-to-air seven-missile launcher, and AK-47 and M-16 rifles.

Naw Kham's close associate Yishe, also ex-MTA, is based at Nampong, west of Tachilek. Needless to say, his main business is also *yaba* and he operates at least one heroin refinery with his deputy Petru. The son of a respected Lahu Baptist preacher in Kengtung, Yishe joined Khun Sa around 1980 and surrendered with the old drug lord in January 1996. Yishe was then authorized to raise his own militia force and he also set up a *yaba* laboratory near Tachilek. During the 2007 Lahu New Year celebrations, Yishe was seen enjoying himself in the company of some lesser known *yaba* and heroin producers—and the local Burmese army commander.

There are also many other smaller operators who are benefiting from the new disorder in Burma's Shan State. But all the *yaba* dealers along the Thai border have to cooperate with the mighty Wei Xuegang, because he is the only one whose chemists can produce a certain white powder, which is made from precursor chemicals and can be refined into "ice," or crystallized methamphetamine. It can also be mixed with caffeine, colorings, and other ingredients, and compressed into pills that are easy to conceal and smuggle across the border.

Laboratory operators in the south have to buy the raw material from Wei in order to make *yaba* tablets, so no matter who the wheelers and dealers are along the Thai border, they all depend on Wei and his network. The pro-government militias and other *yaba* producers on the border have to deal with Wei's pointman in the area, an ethnic Lahu called Kya La Bo, formerly a colonel in the 171 Military Region. This may explain why Wei, and only he, has been able to build a massive, multi-million dollar mansion in the hills. And it has all been paid for by hundreds of thousands of *yaba* addicts in Thailand and elsewhere.

FIVE
THE LAW

IT CAME as no surprise to anyone who had followed developments in the Golden Triangle since the opium boom of the 1990s and the subsequent surge in *yaba* production. At a grand ceremony in New York on January 24, 2005, Roslynn R. Mauskopf, attorney for the Eastern District, or Brooklyn, and Anthony P. Placido, from the Drug Enforcement Administration (DEA), announced the unsealing of an indictment against eight high-ranking leaders of the United Wa State Army (UWSA) on heroin and methamphetamine charges. Present also was Lieutenant General Watcharapol Prasarnrajkit of the Royal Thai Police. In front of the lectern from where the announcement was made the DEA had placed a huge enlargement of a cover of *Time* magazine's Asian edition. It showed a picture of a Wa soldier brandishing a Kalashnikov under the headline "Speed Tribe: Inside the World of the Wa—Asia's Deadliest Drug Cartel." The story was written by two Bangkok-based foreign correspondents, Andrew Marshall and Anthony Davis.

The indictment was the outcome of a long investigation by the DEA and several branches of the Thai police, and it alleged that since 1985 the Wa leaders were responsible for the importation of more than a ton of heroin into the United States. "More recently," a DEA news release said, "the defendants and UWSA began production of methamphetamine for export to the United States and elsewhere. To date, approximately twelve thousand methamphetamine tablets, labeled with the UWSA logo, have been seized by the DEA at mail facilities located within the United States." That logo must have been "WY," the most common mark stamped on pills produced in the organization's *yaba* laboratories. However, many other *yaba* producers also stamp their pills with the same letters, as the mark has gained widespread brand recognition. But the DEA seemed to be sure that the pills seized originated in UWSA-run laboratories.

While the main market for *yaba* has always been in Southeast Asia, small quantities of the drug have been found among Thai communities in California and with Hmong refugees from Laos who have been resettled in the United States. It has not been easy to sell *yaba* in the United States, where it has to compete with locally made or Mexican ice of much higher quality. Among the producers and distributors there are motorcycle gangs such as the Hells Angels; one famous seizure from them in the 1980s netted enough raw materials to produce one ton of the drug, with a street value in New York of about us$1 billion—far more serious than the twelve thousand *yaba* pills seized in us post offices.

But the DEA wanted to make a point, and Wei Xuegang was on top of the list of defendants. He was, allegedly, responsible for smuggling heroin into the United States since 1985 and was first indicted in the United States in 1993. In June 2000 he also became one of the first individuals designated by the United States as a "drug kingpin" under what is termed the Foreign Narcotics Designation Kingpin Act. This time he was indicted along with his two brothers, Xuelong and Xueyin, all four Bao brothers, and an eighth UWSA leader, Bao Hua Chiang, who also goes by the name Ta Kat. He shares the same clan name with the Bao brothers, but is not a relative. According to the DEA's press release, he had at some stage served as a "UWSA trade and finance officer."

The news release also stated that the UWSA "provide[s] security for heroin and methamphetamine laboratories in Wa territory, as well as for drug caravans smuggling heroin and methamphetamine from eastern Burma to Thailand, China, and Laos where independent brokers smuggle shipments to international distribution organizations in Asia, Europe, and the United States." While a us$2 million bounty was promised as a reward for information leading to Wei's capture, each of the others got a price of up to us$500,000 on their heads.

The indictments caused serious concern in the Wa Hills. The United Nations Office of Drugs and Crime (ONODC) temporarily withdrew their international personnel from the area, just in case the UWSA retaliated against foreigners in general. The Wa leaders themselves were upset. They had actually promised to make their area "drug free" by June 2005, but had received very little of the foreign assistance they had previously been offered to offset the effects of the prohibition.

It was probably no coincidence that the UWSA in July 2006—a year after the ban went into effect—appointed Wei Xuegang overall financial affairs chief of the organization. Incomes were down, so they once again turned to Wei and his masterly skills as a narco-mastermind to assist in curbing organizational revenue constraints. And they probably had fewer qualms about being associated with Wei after what they perceived to be a "foreign betrayal."

They did not have to wait long for fortunes to turn. In late 2006, sources close to Wei alleged that he had in October of that year refined three tons of heroin. Most of it was destined for China and India, but some six hundred kilograms were also headed for the Thai border. A few weeks later the trickle effect of this influx could be felt in Chiang Mai as street prices for heroin were reduced—and pure number four heroin was available in abundance from street dealers. By January 2008 the USWA's finances had improved. Wei, "Mr. Remote Control," could retreat into the background and hand over the post, at least officially, to his former deputy, Bao Youliang.

THE UNITED NATIONS OFFICE ON DRUGS AND CRIME— DOING LITTLE TO STEM THE FLOW OF DRUGS FROM BURMA

Various UN agencies have been working in the Wa area since shortly after the 1989 mutiny within the Communist Party of Burma (CPB), and a fifteen-year narcotics elimination plan began in 1999. According to UN figures, the area under poppy cultivation has declined significantly since the program began, with a reported 75 percent reduction between 1998 and 2005. However, while opium production inside the UWSA-controlled area has declined considerably, new poppy fields have been prepared on hillsides in other parts of Shan State. The much touted reduction to 450 tons in 2008 is actually not much of a decline. It may be much less than in the 1990s, but it is still comparable to outputs in the 1970s and 1980s, when 350–500 tons of opium were harvested annually in the Burmese sector of the Golden Triangle. And the "progress" did not extend to *yaba*, the new drug which benefited only the producers and the dealers. Opium, at least, had given impoverished hilltribe farmers some income with which to feed their families.

There is no doubt that many villagers have benefited from the UN's programs in the former CPB areas. Some of them now have clean water and better education, and have been helped to grow crops other than opium. But the approach of the UN's drug officials to the drug problem leaves much to be desired. They tend to treat it as a social and agricultural issue rather than a political problem, and, because they can only work through "host governments," studiously avoid all controversial issues.

The December 2005 "Myanmar Country Profile" issued by the UNODC's country office in Burma, for instance, states that there is in Burma "very little violent crime, not even anecdotal reports of murder, rapes, or kidnappings." The UNODC in Rangoon must have missed the dozens of reports from Amnesty International, Human Rights Watch, and other international human rights organizations that have cataloged widespread extrajudicial killings and systematic rape by the Burmese army.

Amnesty International published as early as May 1988 a detailed report titled *Burma: Extrajudicial Executions and Torture of Members of Ethnic Minorities*. And in 2002 Shan human rights groups compiled a report called *License to Rape*, which details sexual abuses perpetrated by Burma's security forces in the 1990s and 2000s.

According to one of the reported incidents, in July 1994 a group of Burmese soldiers arrived at a village in Möng Nai township in southern Shan

State, where they saw a twenty-two-year old Shan woman resting in a small hut on her rice farm. The troops grabbed her and raped her. After the soldiers had finished, her thirty-eight-year-old mother began to scream loudly, "Burmese soldiers are raping my daughter!" When the soldiers heard this they pointed their guns at the mother and beat her unconscious.

In November 2001, Burmese government troops entered a village in Möng Küng, in central Shan State, and found a fourteen-year-old girl alone at home. Ordering his troops to stand guard outside, the officer of the unit dragged the girl inside the hut and raped her. She cried loudly and he slapped her. Two days after the incident, the young girl's elder sister took her to a hospital in Möng Küng for a medical examination. The girl could not sleep for several days. She wanted to see the officer punished, but there was nothing she could do. Her entire family would have suffered if she had reported the rape to the authorities.

These are just two of more than six hundred testimonies from women and girls who have been raped with impunity by Burmese troops. The Shan documentation of sexual abuse was followed by similar reports from Karen and Chin states, revealing a nationwide pattern of similar violence by the regime's armed forces. Successive reports by the UN's special rapporteurs on human rights in Burma corroborate the findings by local NGOs. The strongest report was delivered by UN special investigator Rajsoomer Lallah in October 2000. He stated that most frequent human rights violations involved extortion, rape, torture, and forced labor, along with summary executions and the forced relocation of people in Burma's minority areas. "Women, particularly members of ethnic minorities, continue to be the subject of torture, rape or inhuman treatment by the military, especially in the context of forcible relocations and forced labor. The perpetrators are reported to benefit from impunity," Lallah reported. But the UNODC has consistently overlooked crimes committed by the regime.

The UNODC has also often turned a blind eye to official complicity in the drug trade. In a December 2002 interview with its in-house magazine published in Bangkok, *Eastern Horizon*, the then UNODC representative in Burma, Jean-Luc Lemahieu, was asked whether the Burmese regime "is structurally involved in drugs, harboring notorious drug traffickers while having its economy fuelled by illicit profits," to which he replied,

"No, the government as an institution is not involved in drugs . . . this does not mean that there are no rotten apples though."

This statement reflects a profound ignorance of how the drug trade works. It is not a question of a "few rotten apples" among Burma's military authorities who may be involved in the drug trade; the UWSA and other militias would never have been able to carry out their activities had it not been for their cease-fire agreements with the government. The role of the military authorities is not to buy and sell drugs but to protect the trade. In return, there is much less fighting in the frontier areas—and proceeds from the trade are reinvested in the mainstream economy, to the benefit of the drug lords as well as the government.

Furthermore, Burmese army units in the field have been told to be as self-sufficient as possible—which means collecting revenue from the drug trade. Since new poppy farms have been established in government-controlled areas of central and southern Shan State, this has meant potentially lucrative income opportunities for the troops in the area. A fifty-six-year-old grandmother from Kengtawng in Möng Nai township in southern Shan State told a Shan researcher in 2007: "They used to tax us in the past. But this year they tax us and they also grow poppies themselves." The grandmother was speaking about the Burmese army's 569 Light Infantry Battalion, which was based near her village.

Since the uprising for democracy in 1988, Burma's armed forces has increased in strength from 190,000 to 400,000 troops, and although it is now equipped with some modern military hardware, primarily from China, the result of this rapid expansion—and the huge amounts of money spent on arms procurement—is that there is not enough money in central coffers to pay for the upkeep of this mighty military machine. In 1996 the Burmese army was forced to institute a self-support system for troops in the fields and their families. The program has involved systematic confiscation of land from local farmers. Military involvement in the drug trade also appears to have grown in recent years, with more taxes on production and the expansion of the army's own poppy fields.

For several reasons, almost a quarter of the new and expanded Burmese army is based in Shan State, prolonging the state of anarchy that has reigned there for decades and causing major hardships for the people.

The benefits provided by the drug trade are undoubtedly a major reason why there are more than 120 infantry battalions in Shan State out of a nationwide total of 528; few other parts of the country can offer similar access to money in order to make the units self-sufficient. In recent years the Burmese army has also benefited from the relocation of poppy fields from the UWSA's area following the 2005 opium ban. Now, most fields are found in central and southern Shan State. But it would also be fair to take into consideration that the most restive resistance to the regime is also in Shan State, which is another reason why there are so many government units based there.

But official complicity in black market activities is not limited to some local units in Shan State and elsewhere. A former Burmese army officer from the central War Office, then in Rangoon, who retired in 2003 to become a businessman told the Shan Herald Agency for News, a Chiang Mai-based news group and research organization, that he used to sign shipping orders in the old capital, getting between 50,000 and 300,000 kyats, or US$50–300, each time. Once he was curious and took a look at the freight on a truck and found a pile of *yaba*. When he reported this to his boss, a former general, he was told: "This is the way of life from the top down through the whole country. How do you think our Senior General Than Shwe, with a monthly pay of 150,000 kyats [US$150], is able to maintain his lavish lifestyle?" Than Shwe's current pay, since April 2006, is 1.2 million kyats, or a little over US$1,000.

Nevertheless, in June 2006 he was able to spend hundreds of thousands of dollars on the lavish wedding of his youngest daughter, Thandar Shwe, to army major Zaw Phyo Win. Video footage of the wedding was leaked to the press and sparked outrage within Burma and outside the country because of the opulence of the ceremony and festivities in Rangoon and the new capital Naypyidaw. According to the website openDemocracy,

> The video—quickly posted on YouTube—revealed a ceremony suffused with classic nouveau riche bad taste, more reminiscent of aristocratic Versailles than of one of the poorest countries in the world . . . It is all there: the overdressed bride, in a gown featuring a Burmese-style tight sarong combined with a western train; the over-abundance of flowers; the canopied

bed; the seemingly never-ending red carpet; the oleaginous announcer wishing the bride and her consort . . . happiness for all eternity. And the highest yuck-point came when the camera focused on the neckline of the bride, her hand delicately adjusting the huge diamonds in a multi-strand jeweled necklace."

Asia World, Burma's biggest conglomerate, headed by retired drug lord Lo Hsing-han and his son Steven Law, is said to have provided the catering, while well-known Burmese tycoon Tay Za's Htoo Trading Company footed the bill for many of the other arrangements. Lieutenant General Myint Swe, commander of Rangoon Division, is thought to have provided the wedding gown.

As for not "harboring notorious drug traffickers," in July 2003 Brigadier General Kyaw Thein, the junta's drug czar, rejected Thai reports that Wei Xuegang was hiding in Shan State. He said he was not even sure Wei was really in Burma at all. It is inconceivable that Kyaw Thein would have been unaware of what most players in the drug trade knew at the time: Wei was busy preparing to move from his base near the Thai border to Nalawt, where he was going to build his new palatial residence. Besides, Major General Thein Sein, then commander of the Burmese Army's Golden Triangle Region Command, had said in a speech before local leaders in Möng La on May 9, 2001: "I was in Möng Ton and Möng Hsat for two weeks. U Wei Xuegang and U Bao Youri from the Wa groups are real friends." In October 2007, Thein Sein was appointed prime minister and he is now the country's fourth-highest ranking general.

Apart from now owning a huge mansion at Nalawt, Wei also has smaller residences in Möng La and in the Bao clan's hometown of Hkwin Ma in the northern Wa Hills—as well a house with an orange orchard at Tawniu-Nam Pateb, ten kilometers east of the Burmese garrison town of Tang-yan, west of the Salween River. In 2001, survey officials in Tang-yan, acting on orders from the local military commander, carved up a two thousand acre plot of land for Wei's Hong Pang company to grow fruit. The land was confiscated and the local people forced to leave. And Wei's business empire has representatives all over the country. He is also most likely a Burmese citizen, otherwise it would have been difficult for him to own businesses and property in Burma. His Burmese name is Sein Win, or "Shiny Diamond."

In September 2001 the *Myanmar Times*, a Rangoon newsweekly, published an article announcing that a company called Hong Pang Group had been awarded a contract "to build a 92-mile (147 kilometer) section of the Yangon (Rangoon)–Mandalay Pyi Daungsu (union) Highway, a project estimated to cost about seven billion Burmese kyats. The Group was one of seven companies which tendered for the contract, and which was awarded by the Ministry of Construction earlier this month."

The Hong Pang Group's Rangoon manager, U Zaw Bo Khant, told the *Myanmar Times* that the company he represented "has been building a highway between Tachilek and Kengtung in Shan State under a project approved by the Myanmar Investment Commission [and] we are also building some of the strategic highways in the Tachilek region."

The *Myanmar Times* went on to describe Hong Pang as "a diversified group with headquarters at Tachilek, [which] is also seeking approval for a gold mining project at Thebeikkyin, in Mandalay Division about 500 miles (800 kilometers) north of Yangon (Rangoon). The company has been negotiating for three months with the Mining Ministry's No. 1 Mining Enterprise to seek approval for the project."

What the paper did not say was that Hong Pang is Wei Xuegang's company, and that it is the largest business conglomerate in the country after the Lo family's Asia World. But the Burmese authorities cannot say whether Wei is in the country or not—and ONODC's Lemahieu is convinced that the Burmese government is not harboring and protecting notorious drug traffickers.

The UNODC and the Burmese authorities—as well as several foreign researchers—usually blame the drug trade on some mysterious and highly secretive Chinese syndicates. Dutch researcher Tom Kramer writes in his book about the UWSA that "Chinese syndicates, not conflict parties such as the UWSA, control the trade." This only echoes the view of Colonel Hkam Awng from the junta's "Central Committee for Drug Abuse Control," who is quoted as saying, "most syndicates are Chinese . . . they have good connections and financing from abroad. It is difficult for us to penetrate their circles."

A recent study, "The Chinese Connection: Cross-Border Drug Trafficking between Myanmar and China" by Ko-lin Chin and Sheldon X. Zhang, two prominent Chinese-American criminologists, challenges the syndicate view: "We have thus far found little evidence to suggest any systematic linkage between drug trafficking and traditional criminal organizations. This observation does not suggest that no individual member of triad societies (Chinese organized crime) was ever part of the drug trade. However, we are fairly certain that triad-type criminal organizations in Hong Kong, Taiwan, or the US are not active players in cross-national drug trafficking operations."

The triads would risk other, more lucrative investments in China if they dealt in drugs. The drug trade from Burma to and through China, Chin and Zhang argue, "is primarily dominated by loosely connected individuals, who operate independently of the syndicates." In fact, any independent operator who wants to manufacture heroin or *yaba* inside the UWSA's territory must get permission from a committee consisting of the top leaders of the organization, mainly Wei and Bao Youxiang and his brothers. For this they pay a fee, and that is how UWSA and its allies finance their activities, apart from income from their own laboratories. And some of that money has to be shared with higher authorities—either in joint ventures between companies established by the UWSA, the former CPB forces in Kokang and Möng La, and the Union of Myanmar Economic Holdings, which is fully owned by the Directorate of Procurement in the Burmese Ministry of Defense, or as gifts to individual officers. In 2000, a militia commander from northern Shan State said that Colonel San Pwint, one of Burma's most feared military intelligence officers, "was showered by so many 'gifts' from both the cease-fire and militia groups that he needed the bank to keep the money for him."

It is unclear how much the UNODC actually knows about corruption in Burma—or, for that matter, about Wei and his activities. After *Time* published its 2002 cover story, ONODC's Lemahieu authored an open letter, refuting its findings and defending his agency's work inside the UWSA-controlled area. But the letter was so riddled with factual errors that he cannot have done his homework before writing it. For instance, he writes about Wei: "To refresh our memory, born in China, his family fled to Shan

State with the KMT (Kuomintang)" but later joined Khun Sa's organization. Thus far, it is correct if ungrammatical, although he refers to Khun
Sa's group as the Möng Tai Army. When Wei joined it, it was called the
Shan United Army and became the MTA only in 1987, after it had merged
with another army and long after Wei had left it.

Lemahieu then goes on to state that Wei joined the CPB in 1974, after
"falling out with Khun Sa." And when "the CPB fell in 1996, he moved along
with the UWSA." Wei never joined the CPB, and the party fell apart in 1989,
not in 1996. Lemahieu concludes by saying that the UNODC "encourages as
many journalists as feasible to visit the Wa and our project zone. Indeed,
nothing beats a personal visit to the project area in order to discover the
discrepancy between the reality within the Wa and the virtual reality of
what is being said and written outside the country."

Lemahieu stops short of defending the UWSA leadership—but a former
consultant to the UNODC, Australian Jeremy Milsom, does exactly that
in his contribution to a book called *Trouble in the Triangle: Opium and
Conflict in Burma*, which was edited by Tom Kramer and two other Dutch
researchers, Martin Jelsma and Pietje Vervest. Milsom, who according
to the introduction "has lived in Burma since 1993," and, therefore, must
be among those who have made many educational "personal visits" to
the Wa Hills, writes: "Wei Xuegang is an interesting figure with respect
to the WSR (Wa Special Region). Having helped the region immensely
both in times of conflict and more recently by being the principal pro-
vider of social and economic development assistance to poor Wa farmers
in the south, there is considerable respect for him. To add to this view
and interestingly, according to senior Wa sources, a condition of Wei
Xuegang joining the UWSA in 1995 was that he not be involved in drug
trafficking any more and work with the WCA (Wa Central Authority) to
help phase out drugs."

The last sentence is puzzling, to say the least, as Wei has been involved
with the UWSA since its formation in 1989. And, after giving up his involvement in the drug trade, Wei appears to have became a philanthropist,
Milsom contends: "Ironically, Wei Xuegang has done more to support
impoverished poppy farmers break their dependence on the crop than
any other single person or institution in Burma, and this has been done

by putting past drug profits back into the people as he perhaps tries to move into the mainstream economy."

Remarkably, Milsom treats the leaders of the UWSA as if they were representatives of the governments of Canada or Norway, taking all their outlandish claims at face value. He even questions whether the methamphetamine production in the Golden Triangle is controlled by the UWSA and its officers. The UNODC, it seems, needs to check on its personnel in Burma. Or, at the very least, encourage them to learn more about the country—and the Was and the geopolitical complexities of local insurgencies and the role of the drug trade in those conflicts—before they depart for their "project zone."

THAILAND: AN UPHILL BATTLE

While the law may have little meaning in military-ruled Burma, and the country's leaders can say what they want without having an independent domestic media to worry about, the situation in Thailand is very different. Corruption exists and is widespread in Thailand as well, but newspapers and magazines regularly report about it. They almost revel in it. Academics study the problem more scientifically. And it is not unusual for officials to be punished for their wrongdoings. There is certainly much more transparency and accountability in Thailand than in Burma, where officials reign with impunity. But, in a Thai context, corruption is also a far more complex issue than in Western countries. There is not one word for corruption in Thai. There are six. Some are tolerated, others are not.

Pasuk Phongpaichit and Sungsidh Piriyarangsan, two leading Thai academics and authors of a book on corruption in Thailand, state that the least severe form of it is called *sin nam jai*, "a gift of good will." This could be a bottle of whisky or some money to a government official who has been helpful. Then comes *kha nam ron nam cha*, "tea money." This is somewhat more severe and could involve money in an unmarked envelope because the person in question wants to get his driving license faster than the usual procedure permits. It could also be a few hundred baht (US$ 1=33 baht) to a policeman who has stopped someone for speeding or reckless driving.

Few Thais would object to those kinds of practices, and it would be hard to find any government official in the country who has not demanded, or accepted, "gifts" and "tea money" from the public and private companies. The bitter reality is that without such gifts few law enforcement oficers would be able to survive. A senior police sergeant, for instance, gets a monthly salary of approximately 10,000 baht, or about US$300. But it gets worse. Thai policemen below the rank of senior sergeant must buy their own guns (they start at 20,000 baht, or around US$600) and many must buy their own motorcycles because of a shortage of government-provided machines. Radios cost officers around 7,000 baht (US$212) each, and all must buy their own uniforms.

Thai police officers just have to look at Malaysia across the southern border to see how disadvantaged they are. Malaysian police officers are much better paid, and uniforms, equipment, housing, and even furniture are supplied by the government. There is corruption among the Malaysian police, too—but on a much smaller scale than in Thailand.

Pasuk and Sungsidh have also pointed out that in the traditional Thai system of government, "officials received their appointment from a higher authority but were not remunerated by any flow of income from the same source. They were expected to remunerate themselves by retaining a reasonable portion of the taxes they collected, and by exacting fees for services rendered."

Today's abysmally low salaries for policemen and local officials are legacies of that old system. They are still expected to find other sources of income. And if that income is excessive, the police officer or civil servant is expected to share it with his or her superiors. Failing to do so can lead to transfer to a lower position or a remote corner of the country.

However, there are more corrupt practices of different kinds in Thailand. The third term for corruption is *praphuet mi chop*, or "improper behavior," followed by *sin bon*, *rit thai*, "bribery, extortion," and *thucharit to nathi*, "dishonesty in duty." The worst form is *kan khorrapchan*, a Thai adaptation of the English word "corruption." The use of a foreign word to describe it shows that it is considered alien and totally unacceptable. It usually involves an immensely rich person or official who is not only taking bribes but lining his own pockets at society's expense.

Corrupt practices also vary from institution to institution. Among the police and civil sectors of the administration the flow of money goes from the bottom to the top. A traffic policeman in Bangkok might stop motorists—especially trucks and other commercial vehicles—and demand bribes to ignore real or imaginary traffic offences. In this way a policeman can collect thousands of baht a day. But he can only keep a small portion of the money in his own pockets. Most of it goes to the chief of his police station, because the traffic policeman wants to make sure that he is not transferred or demoted. The chief, naturally, collects money from all the policemen in his station, and thus ends up with a substantial amount of money—which he, in turn, has to share with his superiors.

This also means that certain police districts in, for instance, Bangkok are more coveted than others by Thai police officers. During the freewheeling days of the Thai economy in the mid-1990s—the heyday of the growing Thai middle class—a trendy magazine, *Caravan*, published a cover story titled "How to buy your own police station." It named Bangrak, in the center of Bangkok where the famous bar street Patpong is located, as the most lucrative. Officers would have to pay their superiors a fortune to be posted there, but then the superior officers would also be able to collect huge sums of money from the street cops, who, in turn, would have to pay weekly visits to the owners of Patpong's go-go bars and sex shows. At the other end of the spectrum were Bovon Mongkol and Pak Khlong Sarn police stations near the Chao Phraya river, which flows through Bangkok. *Caravan* called it "the Siberia where all naughty coppers are sent for punishment." The main excitement there would be the occasional sunken boat or floating cadaver.

Western writers and governments, when writing about corruption in Asia, very often assert that there may be low-level corruption, but there is no evidence that the top is involved. This is a complete misunderstanding of how the system works. The police generals don't stand in the streets and stop motorists, or visit massage parlors to collect monthly "fees" from, for instance, wealthy commercial sex tycoons or sometimes even drug traffickers. But most of the money still ends up at the top of the pyramid, not at the bottom.

Military corruption differs from other forms of malpractice in Thailand. Here, the pyramid is turned upside down. Vast amounts of money are collected in payoffs and "commissions" for arms purchases. But this goes to the top generals, who are responsible for acquiring new weaponry for the armed forces: everything from small arms to artillery pieces, tanks, fighter jets, and naval vessels.

Given the rivalry between different factions within the armed forces, a high-ranking officer needs a support base of loyal followers. So in the military the money filters from top to bottom. A sergeant major in the army is in no position to collect commissions from arms purchases. But support from him and other lower-ranking officers is necessary when a high-ranking officer wants to flex his muscles in a power struggle within the military.

In this environment, fighting the *yaba* menace has been an uphill battle. The temptation to accept bribes from drug traffickers is high. By turning his attention the other way for a while, a police officer can earn the equvalent of several months' salaries in less than a day. And refusing to accept bribes can be dangerous. The traffickers may retaliate, even violently. A high-ranking Thai narcotics intelligence officer once told one of the authors that agents stationed near the Thai-Burmese border would have to be rotated almost every year. "Even the best and most honest cops eventually cave in," the officer asserted.

Furthermore, after pills have been seized policemen have been known to resell them to make some money for themselves. The *Bangkok Post* reported on March 6, 1998, that two policemen and two Border Patrol Police officers in the north had been arrested and charged for having 61,500 *yaba* pills in their possession. They had admitted that the drugs were part of an amount of more than a million *yaba* pills and some heroin seized from a man in the border town of Mae Sai. A year later, a warrant was issued for the arrest of a senior police officer who owned a jeep that had been used in an attempted delivery of 1.02 million *yaba* pills in the north.

The release on bail of prominent drug traffickers, including Wei Xuegang, has embarrassed higher Thai authorities as well. When the notorious Thai drug lord Bang Ron, or Surachai Ngernthongfoo, escaped to Burma in October 1998, several high-ranking police officers were sacked or moved to "inactive posts." Among them was the chief investigator at a police station in Kanchanaburi, who was charged with providing protection for transportation of Bang Ron's drug supplies from the border province to Bangkok on several occasions. Police officers in Bangkok were also punished in connection with the case. In Lam Phak Chi, a suburb of the Thai capital, a chief police investigator was arrested and dismissed for "abuse of authority." He had reportedly helped Bang Ron's gang members when they were arrested on various drug-related charges.

The Thai authorities have repeatedly asked Burma for help in locating Bang Ron and securing his extradition to stand trial in Thailand. In September 2001, Thailand's Office of Narcotics Control Board (ONCB) said it would send arrest warrants and photographs of him to Burma—and to China as well, as the Chinese would most likely have a better idea of his whereabouts. The request was repeated in July 2003, when the justice minister, Pongthep Thepkanjana, insisted that both Wei and Bang Ron were "hiding" in Burma.

The only success, and a sign of some willingness on the part of the Burmese authorities to cooperate with their Thai counterparts, came in May 1997 when Li Yun-chung, a suspected drug-trafficker who had jumped bail in Bangkok and escaped to Burma, was flown back to Thailand. Li has been indicted in the United States in connection with a 486-kilogram heroin shipment to California in 1991.

Having been freed on bail in February 1997, Li was spirited north by a relay of Mercedes cars. He spent one night hiding in Mae Sai, and, disguised as a local trader, was driven across the border bridge into Tachilek in the back of a pick-up truck. From there he went on to Panghsang and was sheltered by the UWSA. Somehow, the Burmese—under immense pressure from the Thais—managed to lure him back to Tachilek, where he was arrested and flown to Rangoon. There he was handed over to the then Thai prime minister, Chavalit Yongchaiyudh, who had arrived in Rangoon on May 16. Intelligence officials saw the Burmese move as a way of pleasing Chavalit, a former general who had been criticized at home and abroad for supporting Burma's ruling junta and for having business interests in the country.

The judge who had granted bail to Li was suspended, and Li was later extradited to the United States. But this appears to be an isolated case. There are several dozen drug traffickers, associates of Wei as well as Khun

Sa, who are wanted in Thailand or the United States, or both, enjoying sanctuary in Burma—usually in the UWSA-controlled area along the Chinese border, which in recent years has become a criminal haven.

In another case, a fugitive who was wanted in the United States for involvement in drug trafficking had to be lured across the border into Thailand to be arrested. In March 1997, Liu Wei Ming, alias Chao Shih, who had been indicted on heroin trafficking charges, was arrested when he sneaked into Chiang Dao district, north of Chiang Mai, and later extradited to the United States. Liu had also been one of the pioneers in the *yaba* trade. A former official in Khun Sa's organization, he had later joined Lin Mingxian's group of the former CPB. A local newspaper in Lin's area had in August 1995 listed him as a member of the newly established "Möng La Action Committee Against Narcotics." In fact, Liu was one of the first drug lords in the Golden Triangle who tried to produce MDMA, or methylenedioxymethamphetamine, which is more commonly known as ecstasy. In the mid-1990s he brought over two Dutch chemists of Chinese origin to manufacture MDMA. However, the most potent mind-altering drug they were able to produce was a high-grade form of "speed," which became known as *ya-ee* (the "*ee*" is for "ecstasy"). It found a niche market in Thailand, but it was not real MDMA.

Corruption in their own country, and lack of cooperation from Burma, are not the only problems facing Thai authorities when dealing with narcotics suppression and fugitive drug lords. Thai narcotics intelligence agencies have excellent, detailed information about traffickers, trafficking routes, and everything else that would be needed to make arrests. But, as we have noticed, their hands are all too often tied because of internal politics and the high-level protection that some drug lords are enjoying. Money is a powerful tool, and the traffickers know how to use it to get maximum benefits for themselves.

How Serious Are the WAs about Giving up Drugs?

The reasons for—and consequences of— the ban on poppy cultivation in areas controlled by the UWSA have been a controversial topic since

Bao Youxiang announced his decision to take such a measure on World Anti-Drugs Day, June 26, 2004. The ban would come into effect a year from the day the announcement was made. Did he really mean it, and wouldn't it undercut the finances of his own organization? It is quite possible that he and other Wa leaders were tired of being branded drug lords by the international community, and that they thought they would get the help they needed to feed the population after the ban went into effect on June 26, 2005. Ordinary Was have actually not much to gain from poppy cultivation, but it had been the way of life for generations. Many farmers did not know how to grow other crops, and the income they got from growing poppies was barely enough to pay for the basic necessities of their families.

But Bao's announcement was, in fact, not a new proposal. In early 1993, Saw Lu, on behalf of the political wing, the UWSP, wrote an open letter to the world community titled "The Bondage of Opium: The Agony of the Wa People, a Proposal and a Plea." It stated: "We want to free ourselves from the slavery of an opium economy. It is in our interest and, we think, in the interest of the rest of the world to stop opium growing. This we cannot do ourselves. Like a heroin addict who wants to 'kick' his habit, we need outside help to be successful." The proposal was also linked to specific political demands, including a separate state for the Was within a federal union, and the restoration of "real democracy for all of Burma."

Saw Lu was an extraordinary character in the UWSP because he had never been a member of the Communist Party of Burma (CPB). Nor was he born in the Wa Hills. He belonged to a Wa Christian community in Kengtung and had studied at the legendary Dr. Sterling Seagrave's missionary school in Namkham in northern Shan State, and later at a Karen-run Bible school in the Irrawaddy delta region.

When the CPB entered the Wa Hills in late 1969 he was a young, local Ka Kwe Ye commander in Saohpa, or Pangwei, in the Wa Hills. He fought against the CPB, which had Wa chieftain Chao Ngi Lai (Zhao Yilai) on its side. The CPB-supported forces with their superior, Chinese-provided firepower drove Saw Lu out of the area, and he settled in Lashio in northern Shan State.

Saw Lu and his Lahu wife Mary ran orphanages and other charities in Lashio. He was also a loyal member of the ruling party at that time, the Burma Socialist Program Party (BSPP). But when the uprising of 1988 swept the country, he and his wife came out in favor of democracy and founded both the Wa National Development Party and the Lahu National Development Party.

Unbeknown to most people, however, Saw Lu was also an important source for the DEA in Rangoon. His work for the drug agency went smoothly, until he was detained by Burmese authorities in January 1992. His arrest was prompted by a detailed report he had compiled about the involvement in the drug trade of Major Than Aye, chief of military intelligence in Lashio. The report was intercepted as it was being sent down to Rangoon. Saw Lu, Mary, their two sons, and two adopted sons were all thrown in jail in Lashio. Saw Lu himself was hung upside down and given electric shock treatment in the presence of Major Than Aye.

On hearing about the arrest, Chao Ngi Lai—then still UWSP chairman—issued an ultimatum: if Saw Lu was not released before March 26, the cease-fire with Rangoon would be over. They might have been old enemies on the battlefield, but their Wa blood ran thicker than ideology, and Chao Ngi Lai considered him a Wa brother. On the sixteenth, Saw Lu was set free. He almost immediately escaped to the Wa Hills, where the UWSA appointed him "official spokesman for international affairs."

Saw Lu's first initiative was to persuade the UWSP/UWSA to accept an opium eradication program that he had worked out while still in Lashio. The Burmese government's so-called Border Development Program, which had been launched shortly after the cease-fire agreement in 1989, had not produced any tangible improvements in the Wa area. The UWSA now appealed directly to the international community. According to their proposal, they needed schools, roads, modern medical care, substitutes for the opium poppy and help to reforest the denuded hills in the Wa area. "We want to focus and highlight our Wa identity," the proposal stated. "We want to give our people what is rightfully theirs but what has been shattered by constant war."

The UWSA, which had much confidence in Saw Lu and his international contacts, sent him to Thailand to meet his foreign friends. Despite what he had been through, he was full of enthusiasm when one of the authors met him in Chiang Mai in May 1993. But the ground-breaking Wa proposal was rejected. The DEA and the UN's various agencies said they were not able to provide any direct assistance to the Was. Any aid would have to go through "proper channels," namely the Burmese government.

Saw Lu returned to the Wa Hills, where people blamed him for the failure in getting direct aid. In 1995 he was relieved of his post and retired to his new home and citrus farm in Saohpa. In the same year, Chao Ngi Lai suffered a stroke, and a new, more business-like Wa leadership under the Bao brothers took over. Then Wei moved some of his operations to Panghsang, bringing with him his particular style of business to the Wa Hills.

The 2005 US indictment of the UWSA leadership may have further alienated the Was from the international community, and they may well have gone back to the defiant attitude that the old Vingngun chieftain Sao Maha had displayed before the frontier areas committee of enquiry prior to Burma's independence from Britain: "We are very wild people . . . we only think about ourselves."

The opium ban went into effect, and two years later there were few poppy fields in the Wa Hills. But the ban caused immense hardships for the indigent farmers. Some turned to growing corn and highland rice, but that could not provide enough food for the six hundred thousand or so people living in the UWSA area, although Milsom claimed in his opus that "the farmers in the region are producing a rice surplus." In reality, rice and other foodstuffs had to be bought in China, or brought in by the UN's World Food Program. After the 2008 Sichuan earthquake and subsequent food shortages China, supplies from there virtually ceased.

Some unemployed Wa poppy farmers found employment in rubber plantations that Chinese investors had established in the hills. Some became *yaba* dealers to make a living. Others simply moved to areas west of the Salween river, where they could grow opium poppies. The Wa Hills may have become opium-free—but they were not heroin-free. Opium harvested in other parts of Shan State was transported into the UWSA-controlled area, where heroin refineries were still in operation. According to the 2007 Annual Report on Drug Control in China, Chinese authorities were involved in 46,300 drug-related cases and apprehended 56,200 suspects in 2006. China seized 5.79

tons of heroin in that year, a 16 percent decrease from 2005 but nevertheless significant. A total of 1.69 tons of opium from Burma was also seized
in 2006, the year after the Wa ban on opium went into effect.

And the trade in ice and *yaba* has continued to flourish, so the drug
hierarchy of the 1960s (described in chapter three) has remained more
or less intact—minus the impoverished hilltribe farmers, who now have
to find other sources of income.

In many ways, the UWSA leadership finds themselves between a rock
and a hard place. On one side are outside forces that have demonized
and indicted them. On the other are ethnic Chinese drug barons such as
Wei Xuegang, who want to maintain the status quo from which they are
benefiting: an area of their own where they can do whatever they want.
In the process, almost the entire UWSA leadership has become hopelessly
corrupt and more interested in business than politics, which Bao Youri
in his Hummer and Bao Youxiang with his bowling alley clearly show.
But, still, the Wa leaders cannot be compared with Wei and his gang, nor
with Lin Mingxian and his ex-Red Guards, outsiders in the area who are
there only for the money.

In the end, it is essential that any sensible approach to the drug problem in Burma includes tackling the political and ethnic issues raised in
Saw Lu's 1993 proposal. It cannot be treated as merely a criminal issue, or
as an agricultural problem, as the UNODC classes it. A lasting solution to
Burma's decades-long ethnic conflicts has to be found before there can
be any end to drug production in the Golden Triangle. The trade in *yaba*
may have an entirely different history than opium and heroin. But the
fundamental ethnic problems that make the trade in the Golden Triangle
possible have not yet been addressed by any Burmese government since
U Nu, or by any international agency. So drugs continue to flow out of
Burma. It is business as usual in the Golden Triangle.

FIGURE 38. The 281-room hotel and casino at "Boten Golden City," Luang Namtha Province, Laos. The casino is owned by Lin Mingxiang and other Chinese investors. *Michael Black.*

SIX

THE BUSINESS

IT IS not only in Burma that remote and once-godforsaken villages have mushroomed into jungle boomtowns. About a decade ago, Boten, the last town in northwestern Laos before the Chinese frontier, received few outside visitors other than car smugglers. Hondas, built at the Japanese motor giant's plant in the United States, or German luxury sedans bought in Bahrain and other Gulf states, were sent to Bangkok and on through Thailand to the northern town of Chiang Khong on the Mekong river. Then they were ferried across to Ban Huay Xay in Laos and driven in convoys to Luang Nam Tha on the border of China's Yunnan province. There, the traders faced Chinese import duties and other charges that could exceed 200 percent of the car's value. But less costly arrangements could be negotiated with the border officials. While the smugglers were waiting for the right moment to cross the border, hundreds of cars were parked on an open field in the middle of nowhere in Boten. Local land-owners earned small fortunes renting out parking space to these rather unusual car dealers.

"Exporting" cars to China via Laos in this roundabout way was a boom-ing business—until the late 1990s, when the authorities on both sides of the border decided to crack down on the racket. But an alternative source of wealth was soon found for this remote border town in Laos. In October 2002, plans for the Boten Border Trade Area were finalized when the coun-try's then prime minister, Boungnang Vorachith, issued a decree to set up a zone for "the promotion of investment, trade and for creating jobs."

The initial plan was later modified, and a twenty-three square kilometer zone was created, which was leased to Chinese investors. Local villagers were told to move out, and their wood and bamboo huts were demol-ished to make way for a three-star, 281-room hotel and casino complex, which opened for business in early 2006. Rates range from US$78 for a standard room to US$2,688 per night for the hotel's presidential suite. All major credit cards are accepted there—and also in the casino, which has nine gaming rooms with around fifty tables offering baccarat at a minimum of 10,000 renminbi (about US$1,450) per hand. Flat-screen televisions that cover one entire wall offer gamblers the opportunity to bet on foreign dog and horse races as well as international sporting events and Formula One competitions. Each of the gaming halls is rented and operated by groups of Chinese investors, although gamblers may come from many different countries. One of the rooms is called the "Korea Club" and, according to local sources, it caters to Korean and Japanese gamblers. Occasionally, Thai gamblers arrive by minibus from Chiang Khong and Ban Huay Xay.

Security guards at the entrance of the main casino confiscate cameras and reading material, which are returned when the gamblers leave. A sign behind the desk prohibits Chinese and Laotian nationals from gambling, although this is clearly not enforced in Boten. Printed signs on the walls seek male and female employees between eighteen and twenty-five years of age, so there are indeed some employment opportunities for local people. Prostitutes are seen roaming the casino looking for customers, but they are exclusively Chinese; no Lao women are in the trade. It is likely that Laos, with its strict laws against prostitution, would have made this a condition in the rental agreements with the investors.

But there are also some other, rather unexpected visitors in this unique free-trade zone in Laos, still officially a socialist country. The number plates on some of the suvs and sedans parked outside the casinos indicate that they come from "Special Region No. 2" and "Special Region No. 4"—the officially designated names for the areas run by the United Wa State Army (uwsa) and the National Democratic Alliance Army (Eastern Shan State) (ndaa [ess]) respectively under the 1989 cease-fire agreements with the Burmese government. One of the main investors in the Boten Golden City, as it is called, is Lin Mingxian.

When the Chinese authorities clamped down on his casino business in Möng La in early 2005, and clearly did not want a similar freewheeling and unregulated gambling town to emerge at Sop Lwe, the ndaa's 911 base, Boten became the alternative for gambling close to the border. The new gaming houses in Möng Ma were accepted because they were sufficiently far away from the border not to irritate the Chinese. But Boten also has certain advantages over Möng Ma, and certainly over Sop Lwe. It is located in a "proper" country, not a gray zone controlled by a private army. Drugs are not tolerated at Boten, and the Chinese can depend on the Laotians to keep an eye on what goes on there; by contrast, the Burmese authorities have little or no say in the former insurgent base areas which have become "special regions," part of Burma but with a high degree of autonomy.

It is uncertain how much money Lin has invested in Boten, but it must be substantial, for nearly three hundred young people from Laos and China have been sent to the gaming houses at Wan Hsieo, near Möng Ma, to learn the trade. Whether that also includes learning the tricks of online gambling is uncertain, but some of the gaming rooms in Boten already have Möng Ma–style video monitors, which could mean that a similar arrangement will be established also at Boten.

The Boten Golden City is just one example of how proceeds from various dubious business activities in the special regions can be laundered or reinvested in what purports to be a legitimate enterprise. But, as is the case with casinos all over the world, those in Boten have also attracted some unsavory characters. The Thai drug fugitive Bang Ron, or Surachai Ngernthongfoo, has reportedly built a huge mansion in nearby Luang Nam Tha and may therefore be in charge of looking after the interests of the special regions in Boten. He travels frequently between UWSA and NDAA (ESS) controlled areas in Burma and northern Laos—and it is fair to assume that it is not for sightseeing.

Bang Ron remains seemingly untouchable, but another of Lin's acquaintances, Burmese tycoon Eike Htun, found himself in serious trouble when the US Department of the Treasury blacklisted his bank on April 12, 2004. According to the official statement, Eike Htun's Asia Wealth Bank and the Myanmar Mayflower Bank, which was founded by another local tycoon, Kyaw Win, were designated as "financial institutions of primary money laundering concern." US citizens were prohibited from dealing with those banks, which were subsequently closed down by the Burmese authorities.

Eike Htun is the subject of one of many mysterious rags-to-riches stories in Burma in the wake of the pro-democracy uprising of 1988—which led to the abolishment of the Burmese Way to Socialism—and, more importantly, the 1989 mutiny in the Communist Party of Burma (CPB). A Sino-Burmese, he sold tea in Rangoon's Chinatown during the Ne Win era, when the country was ruled by the Burma Socialist Program Party. He also drove trucks to make ends meet. But after 1989 he gained some wealthy friends and was able to establish his own bank—and also the Olympic Construction Company, which has invested heavily in residential property and hotel development in Rangoon.

Kyaw Win, the founder of the Mayflower Bank, is also a Sino-Burmese trader with a colorful past. He was born to a poor Chinese family in northern Shan State. In the late 1960s, when he was in his twenties, Kyaw Win worked in Tachilek, where he established ties with local military commanders and business relationships with entrepreneurs across the border in Thailand. One of his close business allies was Thai logging tycoon Choon Tangkakarn, owner of Pathunthani Sawmills. It has been reported that Kyaw Win and some of his Thai business associates operated in the area then controlled by drug lord Khun Sa. This does not mean that they were involved in the drug trade, as Khun Sa's organization also exported timber to Thailand. But it made Kyaw Win rich, and when the Burmese economy opened up in 1988–89 he was able to set up a privately owned company called the Chin Su Plywood Industry. From there he went into banking and became one of Burma's wealthiest men.

The Mayflower Bank was one of Burma's first privately owned financial institutions. It grew to become the third biggest bank in the country and the first to have twenty-four-hour automatic teller machines. But it came under the scrutiny of the investigators of the US Department of the Treasury, who concluded that the bank was involved in money laundering. The official US announcement did not specify what kind of black money the bank had laundered, but the US State Department's 2007 *International Narcotics Control Strategy Report* stated that "Myanmar Mayflower and Asia Wealth Bank had been linked directly to narcotics trafficking organizations in Southeast Asia."

But although their banks were closed down, and despite allegations of connections with the drug trade, no officials from, and no one connected with, either the Asia Wealth Bank or the Mayflower ever faced any charges in a Burmese court.

The Thailand-based NGO ALTSEAN wrote in a 2005 report: "On 31 March, the Ministry of Finance and Revenue announced that their banking licenses had been revoked because banking regulations were not 'strictly followed.' The revocation of licenses for financial institutions is set out in the 'Financial Institutions of Myanmar Law,' and not in [Burma's] 'Control of Money Laundering Law'. Penalties for money laundering offenses, as outlined in the Control of Money Laundering Law include fines and/or imprisonment, not the revocation of licenses."

In other words, as long as regulations are "strictly followed," drug money can be reinvested in the mainstream economy. The chances of being charged with money laundering offenses are minimal. And if bank deposits are declared as winnings from the casinos in Möng Ma or Boten, no questions will be asked. For the merchants of madness, the border casinos and Burma's new banks are essential parts of their business.

HONG PANG—ONE OF BURMA'S BIGGEST AND MOST DIVERSIFIED CONGLOMERATES

"It is the biggest money-laundering operation in Southeast Asia today," a Western narcotics official said in March 1999. Since then, Hong Pang, which means "Prosperous Country" in Chinese, has grown even bigger. And its boss is none other than Wei Xuegang, the man whose whereabouts are supposed to be unknown. Wei directs it from his Nalawt mansion or from his estates in the garrison town of Tang-yan, near the Thai border, and Hong Pang has branches in Kentung, Tachilek, Möng Yawn, and even Rangoon. Over the years, Wei has invested millions of dollars in the lumber business, fruit and vegetable farms, mineral smelting, pig farming, and the retail trade in Burma. His commercial empire also includes a cement factory, gas stations, a drinking water business, pirated CDs and DVDs manufactured in the special regions, and department stores in Lashio, Mandalay, and Rangoon.

He is also widely suspected of having substantial concealed investments in northern Thailand and perhaps also in China. At least in Thailand, where he is wanted by the authorities, he is said to be acting through proxies who own, on his behalf, shares in local companies that are both money laundering and moneymaking operations. At the same time as the Wei and Bao brothers were indicted in the United States in 2005, the US Treasury Department also froze the assets of eleven people and sixteen companies based in Thailand for alleged links with the UWSA. However, the only names that were made public were Warin Chaichamrunphan—Wei's second wife and current favorite—and her brother, Winai Phitchaiyot.

The US indictment against Wei also gave a long list of Hong Pang associated companies in Burma: the Hong Pang Group, the Hong Pang Company, the Hong Pang Import Export Company, the Hong Pang General Trading Company, the Hong Pang Wire and Cable Company, Hong Pang Electric Industry Limited, Hong Pang Agricultural Limited, Hong Pang Textile Limited, Hong Pang Gems and Jewelry Company, Hong Pang Gas and Lighter Limited, and Hong Pang Construction Limited.

Under Hong Pang's umbrella are an additional thirty or so subsidiary companies operating under different names. One is Möng Mau Company, and another is the Greenland Group, which took over Hong Pang's Tachilek offices when Wei was indicted and the Thai authorities requested help from the Burmese to curb Wei's growing economic influence along and across the Thai-Burmese border. But Greenland is just another Wei-owned company, so the change of signs outside the Tachilek office was merely cosmetic. In late 2005, Hong Pang operated briefly under the name Xinghong ("thriving greatness"), but regardless of what name it uses, the company and its ownership remains the same. Wei Xuegang is the boss, and his companion Bang Ron is reportedly in charge of the company's drug network for the Burma-Laos-Thailand tri-border area. Bang Ron belongs to an eleven-man committee that runs Greenland/Hong Pang, with six Thai drug operators working under him. The group has a security force of some five hundred fighters protecting its various branches and executives.

Hong Pang Construction Limited was the branch of his tangled web of companies that was awarded a government contract to pave the Tachilek–Kengtung road, and Hong Pang Gas and Lighter has interests in a gas lighter factory in Burma's northern Sagaing Division. Hong Pang Gems and Jewelry has secured concessions in the jade mine area in Hpakan in Kachin State, and ruby mines in Mogok and Möng Hsu. Precious stones are marketed through another subsidiary, the Good Health Fine Jewelry

Company, which boasts in one of its brochures that it is "the biggest ruby company in the world," and that it "distributes products to the United States, Japan, Thailand, Singapore, Taiwan, Hong Kong and other countries." In 2004, a Chinese magazine reported that the workers in Wei's mines were given *yaba* to work harder—and directed to work naked in order to prevent theft. The Good Health Fine Jewelry has representative offices in Panghsang—and in Yunnan's provincial capital, Kunming.

Most drug traffickers in Burma are also involved in the gem trade—rubies from Shan State and jade from Kachin State—which is almost as lucrative as their own. They regularly attend the biannual gem auctions in Rangoon, which take place in March and October and are hosted by the government-run Myanmar Gems Enterprise, to sell their precious stones—and the traffickers also reportedly use these events to launder drug money. UWSA traders are said to bid on their own gems more than the actual value, which enables them to turn "black" money into "white."

The non–drug-related enterprises no doubt also make money in their own respective fields, but the capital that makes it all possible comes from the drug trade. Wei has not neglected to expand his drug empire as well—and beyond his traditional turf in Shan State. On August 14, 1999, Wei was seen arriving at the Burmese border town of Myawaddy in Karen State, opposite Mae Sot in Thailand. He came with a convoy of sixty trucks, escorted by between 300 and 350 UWSA troops. Prior to the arrival of the trucks, Burmese government troops in the area had stopped all road traffic, claiming "rain damage"—although the actual reason was so that the convoy could pass with less risk of detection. In the town of Myawaddy, Wei set up an office in a two-storey building next to the premises of the local military intelligence unit. A sign outside the office announced that it belonged to the "Wa Peace Troops."

The move to Myawaddy at that particular time was well chosen. In late 1994, one of Burma's oldest rebel groups, the Karen National Union (KNU), had split up. The movement has always been dominated by Christian Karen, but the majority of the rank and file have animist or Buddhist backgrounds. Burma's military authorities managed to use that divide for its own advantage, and in late 1994 some of the Karen Buddhists broke away from the KNU and became the Democratic Karen Buddhist Army (DKBA).

It made peace with the government, and actively assisted the Burmese army when, in late January 1995, it attacked and overran the KNU's jungle headquarters at Manerplaw on the Moei river, which forms part of the border with Thailand.

Supported by the Burmese government, the DKBA started a war against the KNU—and even Karen refugee camps across the border in Thailand came under attack. The alliance with Wei and his "Wa Peace Troops" was meant to strengthen the DKBA's finances and make it self-sufficient. Two months after Wei's visit to Myawaddy, the *Bangkok Post* reported that "Three, possibly four, new laboratories producing methamphetamine pills began operation recently. One is run jointly with the DKBA is in the vicinity of Oo Kay Hta village in Dooplaya, south of the town of Walay."

A few years later, UWSA troops were seen at the Burmese frontier town of Tamu on the Indian border. This was followed by an increasing flow of *yaba* into the adjoining Indian state of Manipur. Not only drugs were sold across the border to India, but also guns. On June 24, 2008, the *Sentinel*, a local newspaper published in northeastern India, reported that the UWSA "is playing a major role in the trafficking of Chinese arms to the Northeast." The weaponry, the *Sentinel* reported, included Chinese-made Kalashnikovs and other automatic and semi-automatic rifles. A number of separatist insurgent groups are active in India's northeast, among them the United Liberation Front of Assam (ULFA) and various factions of the National Socialist Council of Nagaland (NSCN). There is no shortage of customers for guns—or drugs—in India's volatile northeast. And Wei and his men are more than willing to supply both to anyone who wants to buy their deadly wares. The guns are most likely obtained on the black market in China—or through UWSA contacts with officers in the People's Liberation Army—and then resold to buyers in the region.

Wei has also begun to target a new potentially huge market for amphetamine-type stimulants (ATS): Vietnam. In 2008 the UWSA was reported to have become involved in the establishment of industrial-scale laboratories in northwestern Laos, most probably in Luang Prabang or Phong Saly provinces. While some pills are sold in Laos and also smuggled through that country down to Cambodia, Vietnam has a much larger, and more affluent, population. Wei and his associates have been running several *yaba* laboratories in Laos's Bo Keo province since former Thai prime minister Thaksin Shinawatra launched·his war on drugs in 2003. Fearing possible cross-border raids on the laboratories around Möng Yawn, some of the production was moved to a safer environment in Laos, where law enforcement is lax and corruption rampant.

But the recent move of at least two of those laboratories to Luang Prabang or Phong Saly shows that Burma's drug lords want to have direct access into northern Vietnam and urban centers such as Hanoi and Haiphong, and perhaps even more importantly to the southern commercial capital, Ho Chi Minh City, which has reverted to its war-era status as a center for prostitution, wheeling-dealing of all kinds—and drugs.

The new laboratory established on Laos's northeastern border is almost certainly equipped with at least one tablet compressing machine, and is capable of turning out approximately two hundred thousand tablets a day. In the Lao capital of Vientiane, *yaba* retails for 30,000 lao kip (about US$3) per pill, significantly cheaper than in Bangkok, Chiang Mai, and other Thai cities and towns. But Laos is poor, and few young people can afford to pay more for the drug. Moreover, Laos's officialdom is likely cheaper to bribe, so the risks involved are minor. In Vietnam, however, prices are likely to be similar to those in Thailand, where pills sell for 170–200 baht in Chiang Mai and 250–300 baht in Bangkok, or between US$5 and 9.

At the same time, Wei and his associates are continuing their efforts to manufacture ecstasy, which could be an even more lucrative business than *yaba*—if they can get it right. So far, they have not been able do to produce pills of any better quality than those that the men of "Möng La anti-drug activist" Liu Wei Ming manufactured in the mid-1990s. Although they are called *ya-ee* (the "*ee*" is for "ecstasy") they are chemically different from, and notably inferior to, genuine ecstasy imported into Southeast Asia, namely from Europe, which is real methylenedioxymethamphetamine (MDMA) and continues to dominate the high-end user market in the region.

Wei is reported to have employed three chemists from Taiwan to work on his *ya-ee* project. Pills are stamped with a variety of symbols, including an airplane and a Playboy bunny. Once the quality improves, willing consumers of *ya-ee* could be found in northern Thailand—and in Vietnam, where cheaper, mind-altering drugs are becoming extremely popular.

In fact, Vietnam today offers many of the same factors that in the 1990s turned Thailand into a boom market for UWSA-produced ATS. Vietnam has a large population, eighty-five million, with urban youth constituting a growing segment. The country has rising income levels driven by economic growth rates that in recent years have topped 8 percent. As the country develops and urbanization gathers pace, traditional social and political constraints erode—and the demand for drugs increases.

If UWSA marketing and pricing strategies that apply in Thailand are any guide, the coming years are likely to see an expansion of the user base, which is currently centered on discotheques and nightclubs, to include manual workers, students, housewives, and other social groups. It is doubtful whether even Vietnam's harsh anti-narcotics laws—which include a mandatory death penalty for traffickers—will prove up to the challenge of stemming the influx. Wei is bound to become even richer—and Hong Pang will get more money that can be laundered and reinvested in other enterprises.

NOT ONLY HONG PANG

As early as 1989—the year of the first cease-fires—Burma's ruling junta decided that they would no longer confiscate bank deposits and foreign currency earnings of dubious origin deposited locally or brought in from abroad. It opted instead for a "whitening tax" on questionable repatriated funds, levied first at 40 percent and since reduced to 25 percent. Equally significant, in early 1993 de facto legalization of the black-market exchange rate (300–350 kyats per US dollar at the time, as opposed to the official rate of six kyats per US DOLLAR) took place and narco-funds previously held in Bangkok, Singapore, and Hong Kong flooded back into Burma.

In June 1996, the US Embassy in Rangoon released a detailed account of Burma's black economy in its yearly *Foreign Economic Trends Report*. It highlights statistical discrepancies, or what economists call "errors and omissions" in the country's balance of payments. By comparing Rangoon's official trade figures with statistics from a variety of sources—including the United Nations Conference on Trade and Development, the International

Monetary Fund, the Australian National University, and the Centre Français du Commerce Exterieur in Paris—the author of the report discovered US$400 million in unexplained foreign financial inflows during 1995–96, up from US$79 million the previous year.

The economist explained that this was basically money that came into the legal economy but was not recorded by any of Burma's trade partners in official export-import statistics—in short, that it came from smuggling. In addition, Burma spends some US$200 million annually on foreign currency–denominated defense expenditure, which is not recorded in official reports. This, the economist argued, had to be added to the total amount of money in circulation, which cannot be explained in terms of official trade. Thus, the actual amount of money that could not be accounted for in the fiscal year 1995–96 was in fact US$600 million. The real figure was most certainly much higher, but that was all the economist could extrapolate from official statistics.

But why must hundreds of millions in proceeds from smuggling necessarily have been drug money? The answer is that the only two other items Burma produces that could generate large sums of foreign exchange—jade and precious stones—were no longer smuggled to neighboring countries in large quantities. The jade trade was previously in the hands of ethnic Kachin rebels who controlled the mines around Hpakan in Kachin State, from where the jade was smuggled to Yunnan or down to Thailand. But in 1993–94 the government took over the jade mines, and the trade now goes through official channels via Rangoon. The same applies to the gemstone mines in the northeast: mining rights in the region are subcontracted to private entrepreneurs by the military-controlled Union of Myanmar Economic Holdings, which collects duties on the trade.

Six hundred million US dollars may not be a staggering amount by international standards, but in a Burmese context it is significant. According to statistics from the International Monetary Fund, Burma's official export at that time amounted to less than US$1 billion annually, compared to approximately US$2 billion in imports.

That was when Burma was a major heroin exporter. With *yaba* now the main drug flooding the region, drug profits reinvested in the mainstream economy are likely to have become even greater. Additional income from new ventures such as pirated CDs and DVDs, which are produced in the special regions, and the re-export of Chinese weaponry are bound to have generated even more "errors and omissions" in the balance of trade than was the case in the mid-1990s.

Since the 1989 cease-fires, a number of privately owned companies have also benefited, directly or indirectly, from the new arrangements. In 1992 the old drug lord Lo Hsing-han, who had helped negotiate the 1989 cease-fires, and his family set up their Asia World Company. Apart from providing the catering for the extravagant wedding of junta leader General Than Shwe's daughter in June 2006, Asia World has been involved in the import-export business, bus transport, housing and hotel construction, a supermarket chain, Rangoon's port development, and the upgrading of a national highway between Mandalay and Muse on the Chinese border. Its Memorandum of Association under the Myanmar Companies Act identifies Lo Hsing-han and his son Htun Myint Naing, also known as Steven Law, as major shareholders. Other shareholders include individuals who are closely associated with drug traffickers from Kokang. In 1996 Steven Law was refused a visa to the USA on suspicion of involvement in narcotics trafficking.

Other companies with suspected drug connections include the Peace Myanmar Group, a rapidly expanding business empire controlled by the Yang brothers from Kokang. Both Yang Maoliang and Yang Maoan are listed in several US State Department reports as major drug traffickers—and their younger brother Yang Maoxian was arrested in China on drug trafficking charges in 1994, and executed in Kunming. Their company used to hold the franchise for Mitsubishi Electric in Burma, and it operates a paint factory and liquor distillery producing well-known brands such as Myanmar Rum and Myanmar Dry Gin. It also has a large consumer electronics showroom on Merchant Street in Rangoon, a joint venture with the Ministry of Commerce.

The World Group of companies is owned by Wa interests and has investments in construction, retail trading, import-export, and the tourist industry. Another Wa-controlled company, the Myanmar Kyone Yeom Group—which once ran a finance company that foreign analysts described as a "thinly disguised money-laundering vehicle"—fell out with the government in 1998, and its chairman, a former UWSA colonel, escaped to Thailand.

But it is not all drugs. The Wa leadership has even tried to promote tourism in its area, and it published a brief guide for travelers who want to visit Special Region No. 2. The guide features pictures of hotels and nightclubs in Panghsang, Buddhist pagodas, Chinese-style pavilions, and jewelry shops. Another brochure, this time from the Panghsang Entertainment Company, attempts to lure tourists to the UWSA's unofficial capital with a range of other attractions: a temple dedicated to the revered Chinese goddess of unconditional love, compassion, and mercy, Guan Yin; an exciting bat cave; supposedly no less engaging transvestite shows; and "a British-style solar observatory," although the brochure does not explain what that is. Tourists in Panghsang can also pay a visit to an equally mysterious "haunted house."

It is uncertain how many foreign visitors Special Region No. 2 managed to attract, but could not have been many. The only Westerners allowed in are UN officials, a small number of foreign NGO workers, and a few invited guests. The area remains basically off-limits to foreign visitors.

But the border town of Tachilek is more easily accessible, and there the UWSA and its associates are said to have interests in a local golf club and a casino resort, and effectively control a hotel in the town center, where a sign in a lobby tells visitors not to bring durian fruit or hand grenades onto the premises. Signs posted around town bring messages such as, "Welcome to Tachilek, City of the Golden Triangle," "Join us in the peaceful eradication of psychotropic substances," "Narcotics traffickers will be severely punished"—and "The Tatmadaw [Burmese army] is your mother and your father. If you cannot trust your mother and father, who can you trust?" With all the drug money around Tachilek, and sign boards indicating that drugs are not welcome, it must be hard for the people of the town to trust anybody.

The Good Shan Brothers International Ltd. is controlled by the family of the late drug lord Khun Sa. In February 1996, a month after his surrender to the central government, ten new companies were registered at an obscure address in Rangoon, a virtually empty room in a town house with little more than a sign and a mailbox outside. The registered owner of the premises is the Good Shan Brothers, which is engaged in "export, import, general trading and construction," according to the official Myanmar Business Directory. In two surprisingly candid interviews with a correspondent from the Austrian daily *Die Presse* in 1997, Khun Sa stated that he was investing in real estate, the hotel business in Rangoon, and a new motorway from Rangoon to Mandalay. Even before Khun Sa died in October 2007, his sons had also invested in casinos in Tachilek. One of his daughters looks after the family's business interests in northern Thailand. However, none of Khun Sa's children attended the funeral ceremony for the late warlord, which was held a few weeks after his death at his old stronghold of Ban Hin Taek in northern Thailand. They feared being arrested by the Thais if they had showed up.

At Khun Sa's old headquarters at Homöng, near Thailand's northwestern frontier, some of his ex-followers set up the Shan State South Company in April 1999. Homöng, as well as the firm, is run by a six-member committee appointed by Burma's military government. By 2000 its businesses were doing well. It ran long-distance buses and was involved in the construction of a hydroelectric power plant in Shan State. The Burmese authorities allowed it to import 250 four-wheel-drive pick-up trucks for business use and agreed to provide it with five thousand gallons of petrol per month for its trucks. Shan State South was involved not only in construction; it was reported in the Thai press in August 2000 that the firm had at least two *yaba* factories in Homöng, capable of producing millions of pills. Khun Sa's favorite son, Sam Heung, was one of the six members of the committee.

Lin Mingxian is widely believed to own the Shwe Lin Star Company ("Golden Lin"), which reportedly has representatives as far afield as Singapore, Malaysia, and Hong Kong. According to a January 2005 report compiled by the Lahu National Development Organization, an ethnic Lahu NGO based in Thailand, Lin's companies are "often favored for government construction contracts in Burma." In 1997, Burma's then intelligence chief, General Khin Nyunt, presented Lin with an "Outstanding Social Activist Award" after declaring his territory a "drug-free zone."

Having established himself as a casino tycoon, first at Möng La and then at Möng Ma and Boten, Lin is about to embark on an even bigger venture: he and some Chinese investors are involved in an estimated

US$200 million casino project at Ban Huay Xai in Laos, near Bankwan, the scene of a bitter battle between Khun Sa and Nationalist Chinese Kuomintang forces in July 1967. Khun Sa had tried to conduct a massive, sixteen-ton opium convoy directly into Laos, bypassing the KMT's checkpoints and tax gates along the Thai-Burmese border.

Khun Sa was ambushed and had to retreat, and the rest is history. Now more peaceful times prevail, and the Ban Huay Xai casino will be conveniently located just across the Mekong river from Thailand—close to a newly completed highway. Thousands of Chinese worked on that road project, which was financed by the Asian Development Bank and now connects Ban Huay Xai with Boten and the Chinese road network. A bridge is planned to replace the current ferry crossing between Ban Huay Xai and Chiang Khong in Thailand. This will be China's main overland connection with Southeast Asia—offering ample opportunities for Lin to become even richer.

As speculated, Naw Kham's attack on the Chinese patrol boat in February 2008 may have been an attempt to get at money destined for this project, which includes two mega-casinos. When it is finished, gamblers will be able to visit casinos on both ends of the new road from China to Thailand, and it is doubtful that Naw Kham, basically a petty border bandit, will be able to interrupt the project by demanding money from people traveling through what he considered his turf.

Lin's company and all the others in the northeastern border areas have to be in partnership, directly or indirectly, with the Union of Myanmar Economic Holdings (UMEH), Burma's biggest holding company, 40 percent of which is owned by the defense ministry's Directorate of Defense Procurement, with the rest belonging mainly to senior military personnel and their families. Known locally as the U-Paing Company, it is involved in the gems trade, banking, logging, timber processing, and coal mining, and it is the joint-venture partner in several projects involving foreign investment. Officially, its capital comes from the Burmese army's pension funds, but various drug lords have invested heavily in this firm, often in partnership with high-ranking army officers.

Jane's Intelligence Review concluded as early as March 1998 that "The repatriation and laundering of narco-profits as well as the impunity enjoyed by the barons has clearly become institutionalized: a 'don't-ask' policy over the source of funds used by Burma's new generation of narco-capitalists has been adopted at the highest level of government . . . the reality is a creeping criminalization of the economy: narco-capitalists and their close associates are now involved in running ports, toll roads, airlines, banks, and industries, often in joint ventures with the government. No less disturbing is the military regime's growing dependence on narco-dollars to keep a desperately floundering economy above water. This wary but mutually beneficial relationship between the junta and the narco-barons is a habit that is likely to prove even harder to break. Ultimately, the survival of both may depend on it."

Cyclone Nargis Shakes Burma

In the first week of May 2008, a cyclone that became known as Nargis devastated the Irrawaddy delta, Burma's rice bowl and home to millions of farmers. At least 130,000 people were killed and 2.4 million made homeless or affected in other ways. It was the worst natural disaster in Asia since the December 2004 tsunami. More than 40 percent of those affected were children—in a region where young people already suffered from malnutrition. Drinking water was in short supply, as most sources had been contaminated by decomposing corpses. Entire villages were wiped out with hardly a building standing—except for the Buddhist temples, which were usually built with stronger materials than ordinary wooden houses. Crops were destroyed by saltwater seeping into the fields, which may have a devastating long-term impact on the country's food supply.

The world wanted to rush to assist the victims—but the country's military government responded by retreating into its shell and turning down offers of help. The us amphibious assault ship uss Essex was moored off Burma's southern coast, while the French naval ship Le Mistral waited in the same waters. Tens of thousands of gallons of drinking water, ambulances, heavy trucks, and medical teams could have reached Burma within an hour by helicopter and landing craft from the uss Essex. Le Mistral carried a cargo of one thousand tons of food—enough to feed at least a hundred thousand people for two weeks—as well as thousands of shelters for the homeless.

Having waited for weeks, both ships eventually had to leave when the Burmese government refused to let them bring their goods ashore. Private Burmese citizens who had organized relief efforts were arrested, and the people told to fend for themselves. The official newspaper, the *New Light of Myanmar*, assured its readers that hunger would not be a problem, since farmers could gather water clover or "go out with lamps at night and catch plump frogs." And to show that the government was on top of the situation, planning minister Soe Tha stated in a truly Orwellian manner that "665,271 ducks, 56,163 cows and 1,614,502 chickens have been lost in the storm—along with 35,051 acres of fish ponds and 22,200 metric tons of beef."

Only after severe pressure from the international community, including the United Nations and Burma's neighbors and fellow members in the Association of Southeast Asian Nations (ASEAN), did the regime allow some aid to reach the victims. But all efforts were strictly supervised by the country's military authorities, and the movement of aid workers severely restricted.

The world was flabbergasted. How could any regime do this to its own people? It was a natural disaster with no one to blame, and the aid that was offered came with no strings attached. But from the junta's perspective, it made some obscene sense. If foreign troops—which should have overseen the distribution of supplies—had entered Burma, their presence could have emboldened the country's citizens to launch yet another uprising against the regime. Ordinary Burmese were already angered because of a bloody crackdown on pro-democracy demonstrations led by Buddhist monks in September 2007. If anti-government activists thought they could count on foreign protection—even if the foreign troops were in Burma on a purely humanitarian mission—they could have taken to the streets again. Hence, troops from foreign countries that have criticized the regime and expressed support for Burma's pro-democracy movement had to be kept out at all cost, no matter how much food and medicine they could have supplied.

The September 2007 movement was the most massive popular manifestation against the regime since the 1988 uprising. Tens of thousands of monks led demonstrations in the old capital Rangoon and some other towns and cities across the country. Thousands of ordinary Burmese from all walks of life joined the marches, calling for an end to military rule. It all began when, without warning, the government raised fuel prices in August of that year. The Buddhist clergy joined the protests when troops fired warning shots and used tear gas to disperse a demonstration led by monks in Pakokku, a town in the central Burmese plains.

The military responded in the same way it always had: by sending in the troops. Soldiers and riot police clubbed and teargassed protesters—and opened fire on monks and demonstrators. A Japanese photographer was among those killed in the streets of Rangoon that September. The regime's official figures put the death toll at ten people, but up to two hundred are believed to have been killed during the crackdown.

The US government, one of the junta's fiercest critics, almost immediately slapped sanctions on Burmese government officials and their business cronies. Among them was the powerful, forty-four-year-old tycoon Tay Za, who is close to junta leader General Than Shwe and his family—and who picked up most of the bill for the general's daughter's lavish wedding in June 2006. His Htoo Trading Company was one of the main contractors that built Burma's new administrative capital, Naypyidaw, where the administration moved in late 2005. An entirely new city was constructed in what basically had been jungle near the central town of Pyinmana. Tay Za also has his own airline, Air Bagan, which was sanctioned by the US government along with Htoo Trading in Burma and its subsidiaries in Singapore.

Tay Za has never been associated with the drug trade—unlike Tun Myint Naing, or Steven Law, the son of Lo Hsing-han, who was in charge of catering for Than Shwe's daughter's wedding. His company, Asia World, was added to the US sanctions list on February 25, 2008. According to an announcement by the US Department of the Treasury, "Lo Hsing-han, known as the 'Godfather of Heroin', has been one of the world's key heroin traffickers dating back to the early 1970s . . . Steven Law joined his father's drug empire in the 1990s and has since become one of the wealthiest individuals in Burma." On the same day, President George W. Bush commented on the decision to sanction the Lo family and their companies: "The Department of the Treasury has applied financial sanctions against Steven Law, a regime crony also suspected of drug trafficking activities, and his financial network."

The Asia World group of companies includes Asia World Port Management, which is in charge of a terminal at Rangoon's new deepwater port at Thilawa. Its branch specializing in construction was the other main contractor that built Naypyidaw. Asia World has also built a US$33 million toll highway from Lashio to the Chinese border, and has been involved in the renovation of Rangoon's international airport. Lo's companies also have a subsidiary in Singapore, Golden Aaron Pte Ltd, which was on the list of companies sanctioned by the US treasury department.

Two of Burma's biggest conglomerates—Htoo Trading and Asia World—seemed doomed. But Cyclone Nargis came to the rescue. The Burmese government did not want any aid for the victims, but at a donors' conference in Rangoon in May 2008 it asked the international community for US$11.7 billion dollars for "reconstruction" of the delta. It had already entrusted the task to some regime-friendly enterprises—among them Htoo Trading and Asia World. Tay Za's company would undertake reconstruction work in Kyngyungone Township under the direction of Brigadier General Hlun Thi, while Asia World was awarded a contract to rebuild destroyed houses, government buildings, and schools in Bogalay and other parts of the delta. The Lo family enterprise would be working there under the guidance of forestry minister Brigadier General Thein Aung.

It is highly unlikely that the Burmese government will get billions of dollars in aid, especially with its choice of contractors. But it shows how little the government in Naypyidaw cares about international opinion, whether because of its handling of a natural disaster or its complicity in the drug trade. Without the protection of the government it would be impossible for companies such as Asia World—and Hong Pang, Shwe Lin Star, Shan State South, the Peace Myanmar Group, the Panghsang Entertainment Company, and a long string of others—to function and operate freely. Burma today has become a country where the drug business is an integral part of the mainstream economy and one of the country's most lucrative growth industries. And it is spreading its wings into neighboring countries other than Thailand, making it a problem that should be of regional concern.

SEVEN
THE FUTURE?

A NEW town has been built in the lush hills northeast of Mandalay. It is located near the British-built hill station of Maymyo, where, during the hot season in March to May, the colonial administrators went to escape the heat and dust of the plains. Maymyo still boasts red brick mansions covered in ivy, and pleasant gardens with roses and other flowers and plants, which flourish in the almost alpine climate of the hills.

The new town is also a kind of refuge—but this time for the Burmese military. There are no Victorian-style mansions here, just gaudy luxury villas. When the construction began in late 2005, the *Irrawaddy*, a magazine published by Burmese exiles in Thailand, reported that "no expense has been spared to allow the generals to live in what basically is a resort, complete with an artificial beach and a man-made stretch of water to lap onto it."

The theme-park resort will also include replicas of famous pagodas in Rangoon and the old royal palace in Mandalay, as well as a model of the popular beach resort of Chaung Tha on the sea southwest of Rangoon, which, the *Irrawaddy* said, "is probably where the fake beach comes in." The choice of Maymyo, which the generals have renamed Pyin U Lwin, as the location for the new resort town was hardly a coincidence; it is also home to the Defense Services Academy, Burma's "West Point," where many of the ruling generals were educated, and where the next generation of military leaders is being groomed.

In early 2007, construction of a cybercity began close to the generals' resort. Seven thousand acres of land were confiscated from its owners by the army to build a complex combining a software-based industrial zone with even more luxury residential areas. The small airport in Maymyo has also been upgraded to facilitate flights to the new capital, Naypyidaw, which means "Royal City" or "Abode of Kings"—and that is how the Burmese generals view themselves. They have decided to change Burma forever and establish an entirely new kind of state built on ideas that are very different from those on which the country was formed as a federal union in 1948.

The creation of a new national concept for Burma began when, on May 27, 1989, the official name of the country was changed to Myanmar. "Burma," for reasons that are historically absolutely incorrect, was termed a "colonial name," and therefore had to be abandoned. But historical accuracy was not an issue for the generals. A cultural revolution had begun, and a military-appointed commission was tasked with the rewriting of Burmese history to suit the new power-holders.

It was not only the country itself that was given a new official name—although it has always been *myanma naingngan* or *bama pyi* in Burmese. Rangoon became Yangon, and even more offensive were name changes in the ethnic minority areas, especially in Shan State. Pang Tara, Kengtung, Lai-Hka, Hsenwi, and Hsipaw—place names that have a meaning in Shan—have been renamed Pindaya, Kyaingtone, Laycha, Theinli, and Thibaw, which sound Burmese but have no meaning in any language.

Dutch Burma scholar Gustaaf Houtman calls this development the "Myanmafication of Burma," which he describes as a move away from the original idea of a federation—agreed by Aung San and the leaders of the ethnic minorities at the Panglong conference in February 1947—to the new "Myanmar" identity propagated by the junta.

The path forward for junta leader General Than Shwe—and, indeed, his vision for this new state of "Myanmar"—became clear on March 27, 2006, in the new capital. March 27: Burma's Armed Forces Day. It was meant to commemorate the day in 1945 when the Burmese nationalists, led by Aung San, shifted sides, joined the Allied powers, and took up arms against their former patron and benefactor, the Imperial Japanese Army. But addressing a crowd of twelve thousand soldiers, Than Shwe said: "Our Tatmadaw [armed forces] should be a worthy heir to the traditions of the capable *tatmadaws* established by noble kings Anawratha, Bayinnaung and Alaungpaya."

None of them had fought the Imperial Japanese Army—they were old warrior kings who had established Burmese empires. In AD 1044 Anawratha founded the first of those empires and established a new capital at the temple city of Pagan on the banks of the Irrawaddy River, southwest of today's Mandalay. He conquered Thaton, the capital of the Mon—major rivals of the Burmans for control of the central plains—and expanded his empire down to the Andaman Sea.

Bayinnaung was Burma's most celebrated warrior king. He reigned from 1551 to 1581 and conquered territories north of Pagan, parts of the Shan plateau in the east, and pushed as far east as Chiang Mai in today's northern Thailand and Vientiane in Laos. He was the most prominent ruler of the Second Burmese Empire and ruled from Pegu in the central plains.

Alaungpaya reigned in the eighteenth century and was the first king of the Konbaung Dynasty, the third and last of the Burmese Empires. Alaungpaya also fought the Mon, and his successor, Hsinbyushin, sacked the Thai capital of Ayutthaya in 1767, a deed for which the Thais have never forgiven the Burmese. But the Konbaung kings were defeated by the British in the three Anglo-Burmese wars of 1824–1826 and 1885, and the country became a British colony. In 1885, Thibaw, the last king of Burma, was led away by the British in front of a mourning and wailing crowd who had come to take farewell of the last monarch of an independent Burmese state. He was sent with his once-powerful wife, Supayalat, and their children into exile in Ratanagiri in India, where he died in 1916.

On the Naypyidaw parade ground stand newly erected, larger-than-life statues of these three warrior kings, whom Than Shwe sees as his role models—and he has also formed not only a new capital but a new Burmese state: the State of Myanmar, a unitary state that is fundamentally different in nature from Aung San's concept of "unity in diversity," federalism, and some kind of parliamentary democracy. In "Myanmar" everybody is a "Myanmar," and a subject of the new King in Naypyidaw. There are no portraits of Aung San in Naypyidaw.

The new State of Myanmar became official when millions of people in southern Burma's coastal areas were reeling under the devastation of Cyclone Nargis. On May 10, 2008, a referendum was held on a new constitution, which would secure a leading role for the military in governing the country. Critics all over the world urged the Burmese government to postpone the referendum and allow foreign aid workers into the worst affected areas in the Irrawaddy delta. Both exhortations were ignored. The referendum was postponed only in forty-seven disaster-hit townships in the Irrawaddy and Rangoon Divisions—and, if official figures were to be believed, 92.4 percent of voters approved the charter, with a 99 percent turnout. Two weeks later, on May 24, voters in Yangon and the Irrawaddy Delta affirmed the constitution by an even more resounding 92.93 percent, the state-run *New Light of Myanmar* newspaper reported.

But there were few who took those announcements seriously. The official version of the outcome of the referendum was repudiated by most Western countries and international advocacy groups. Human Rights Watch reported:

> The government-controlled media offers only crude propaganda in favor of a "Yes" vote, and talks of criminal penalties for those who oppose the referendum, creating a climate of fear. There has been no critical public discussion of the constitution's contents; most people have not even seen the document. The generals are sending a clear message that their hand-crafted constitution will continue the military rule that has persisted for more than four decades.

BURMA'S CEASE-FIRE AGREEMENTS IN DANGER OF UNRAVELING?

As usual, international criticism had no effect on Burma's recalcitrant generals. They were firmly entrenched in power and had no intention of giving it up, or even sharing it with anybody. Within weeks of the referendum, the cease-fire groups came under renewed pressure to surrender their arms. The leaders of the Shan State Army-North were told to retire and form a political party, while the soldiers were to be integrated into the Burmese army. In July 2008, Lin Mingxian's group at Möng La came under similar pressure, while the United Wa State Army (UWSA) was told to withdraw its forces from areas southeast of Panghsang—that is, from Lin Mingxian's area—and to transfer the local administration to the Burmese army.

The response from the cease-fire groups was to adopt a wait-and-see attitude. But it is clear that they were preparing for a possible resumption of hostilities even before the controversial referendum—with assistance from China. *Jane's Intelligence Review* reported in its March 2008 issue: "As the possibility of a war with the junta has loomed larger, the UWSA has acquired more sophisticated weapons, including anti-aircraft systems. In or around 2000, the Wa added to their small arsenal of Soviet Strela-2 (SA-7) man-portable air defense systems when they acquired HN-5N systems, an improved Chinese version of the first-generation Soviet system."

In addition, the UWSA have acquired 12.7 and 14.5 mm anti-aircraft guns as well as 60 mm, 82 mm, and 120 mm mortars. In 2007, advisers from the Chinese People's Liberation Army (PLA) provided training in the use of 122 mm and 130 mm artillery in the Lu Fang mountain range west of Panghsang. The UWSA's artillery regiment has been equipped with 130 mm field guns and 122 mm howitzers, and its soldiers have dug a complex of underground command centers near Panghsang, clearly intended for protection against aerial attacks by the Burmese air force.

The possibility of renewed hostilities between the cease-fire groups and the central government moved closer to reality when, in October 2004, Burma's until then powerful intelligence chief, General Khin Nyunt, was purged and subsequently arrested. Khin Nyunt's ouster was not, as some reports in the foreign media at the time suggested, a power struggle between the "pragmatic" intelligence chief and "hardliners" around General Than Shwe and his deputy, General Maung Aye. According to the press reports, Khin Nyunt favored a dialogue with the country's pro-democracy movement and held "moderate" political views. Khin Nyunt may have been smoother in his dealings with foreigners, but his dreaded military intelligence service, the Directorate of the Defense Services Intelligence (DDSI), was the junta's primary instrument of repression against the pro-democracy movement. During the August–September 1988 uprising he had cracked down on the demonstrators and had student activists imprisoned, tortured, and even killed.

A more plausible explanation for the purge was that Khin Nyunt and his DDSI had accumulated significant wealth through their involvement in a wide range of commercial enterprises—and with close links to the UWSA and other cease-fire groups. Khin Nyunt and his men were building up a state within a state and not sharing their riches with the rest of the military elite. And Than Shwe did not want to have any potential rivals around him; Khin Nyunt also clearly had political ambitions. He was a man not to be trusted.

Immediately following the ousting of Khin Nyunt, his latest intelligence outfit, the Office of the Chief of Military Intelligence (OCMI), was dissolved and an entirely new organization established: the Office of the Chief of Military Affairs Security (OCMAS), which was placed under more direct military control. Details of the new military intelligence apparatus remain sketchy, but it is not believed to be as efficient as its predecessors. Some observers even argue that the regime's inability to prevent the emergence of a massive anti-regime movement in September 2007 would not have been possible had Khin Nyunt and his men remained in charge of security.

And it was Khin Nyunt who had negotiated the cease-fire agreements with the former CPB forces and other rebel groups in 1989. Within days of his ouster, Burmese military leaders met with the cease-fire groups, asserting them that nothing was going to change—but that was not quite the case. In Panghsang and other UWSA strongholds, posters with pictures of Khin Nyunt and Bao Youxiang walking hand in hand were taken down. *Yaba* laboratories on the Thai border were moved to more secure locations near Panghsang. It was clear that relations between the cease-fire groups and the central government were deteriorating. The central government would have liked to see the cease-fire groups disarm and transformed into political parties and "local police forces"; the Was and other ethnic groups had no intention of giving up what they had gained through decades of fighting and the 1989 agreements with the central government.

China's policy towards the UWSA—and Burma—is by no means clear-cut. On the one hand, it supports the government in Naypyidaw and has blocked Western attempts to bring the Burma issue to the attention of the UN's Security Council. But, on the other, Beijing clearly sees a strategic benefit from maintaining a buffer zone between its border and Burma's characteristically erratic ruling generals, and it has various strategic and economic interests in maintaining the UWSA's dominance over the area. Many of the special regions are also administered by former Communist Party of Burma (CPB) commanders, with whom China has a long-standing relationship. Most prominent among them is, of course, the former Red Guard Lin Mingxian, but the Bao brothers, the local leadership in Kokang, and even the ex-CPB force in Kachin State, the New Democratic Army, have always been close to China.

Beijing also fears that a weakened UWSA could invite the Burmese army to launch an offensive, which would risk spilling into China's adjacent Yunnan province and have the potential to create a refugee situation similar to that in Thailand, where more than one hundred thousand ethnic Karen, Karenni, and Mon have sought shelter from Burma's civil war.

It is unclear if the UWSA had to pay in full for its new Chinese weapons, or if they were sold at friendly prices by the PLA. But in order to raise money for arms purchases and to run its administration, the UWSA has also moved into regional arms trade. Until recently, most of the arms the UWSA sold to other regional insurgent groups were procured through Yunnan's underground markets, where ex-PLA personnel are known to have sold off munitions stockpiles without Beijing's approval. These activities intensified in Yunnan in the wake of Beijing's ambitious modernization campaign for its armed forces, which included strict orders for provincial PLA members to abandon their private business interests, including arms trading.

While various PLA units were reshaped and re-equipped, many others, particularly in far-flung Yunnan, were reluctant to hand in officially retired arms because of their black market value in conflict-ridden neighboring Myanmar. The UWSA has long been involved in the lucrative underground regional arms trade, which according to security analysts has surpassed Cambodia's notorious arms bazaars in trade volume. In recent years the UWSA is known to have sold assault rifles and explosives to various rebel groups, including the Naga along India's northeastern border with Myanmar, and possibly also the Maoist rebels who in 2008 fought their way into government in Nepal. Said one Bangkok-based security analysts monitoring the situation: "The UWSA couldn't care less about the various ideologies of the groups they supply. They will continue to sell [arms] to whoever wants them as long as they don't expect to face off with the buyers in the near future."

The June 2008 article in the northeast Indian newspaper *Sentinel* quoted an Indian intelligence source as saying that Chinese automatic rifles, which are available in Burma for US$500 each, are sold in northeastern India for US$2,500 a piece.

The UWSA's attempts at strengthening its finances by diversifying its commercial activities thus represent a clear threat to regional security—quite apart from the menace caused by the continuing flow of drugs into Burma's neighboring countries. But so far only the West seems to be interested in the issue. None of Burma's energy-hungry neighbors wants to antagonize the regime in Naypyidaw, which is sitting on a wealth of natural gas. Thailand is already a buyer, and China has also invested in Burma's energy sector, apart from benefiting from a booming cross-border trade in consumer goods.

To counter China's influence, India has moved from supporting Burma's pro-democracy movement—which it did after the 1988 uprising—to wooing the generals. In October 2007 Satya Sagar, a critical Indian writer, wrote on his website:

> Of all the countries around the world the most shameful position is held by India, once the land of the likes of Mahatma Gandhi but now run by politicians with morals that would make a snake-oil salesman squirm. India likes to claim at every opportunity that it is 'the world's largest democracy' but what it tells no one, but everyone can see, is that its understanding of democracy is also of the 'lowest quality.' Why else would the Indian government for instance send its Minister for Petroleum Murali Deora to sign a gas exploration deal with the military junta in late September [2007] just as it was plotting the wanton murder of its own citizens? In recent years India, among other sweet deals, has also been helping the Burmese military with arms and training—as if their bullets were not hitting their people accurately enough . . . The 'pragmatic' phase of Indian foreign policy toward Burma since the early nineties meant throwing principles out the window and doing anything required to further Indian strategic and economic interests."

The Association of Southeast Asian Nations, ASEAN, sticks to its principle of non-interference in the internal affairs of its member states, which means that the situation in Burma is hardly discussed at their meetings. ASEAN did issue a statement after the crackdown on the monks in September 2007, calling the military government's action "repulsive." But soon it was back to business as usual—and the drug trade, which affects the entire region, has never been seriously discussed at ASEAN meetings. Again, regional security and political concerns weigh heavier than the well-being of all the young and old people who have become addicted to *yaba*.

But given the devastating impact of the trade in drugs—and now also arms—it can hardly be considered an "internal Burmese affair." And if the cease-fire agreements were to unravel, it would have an even greater impact on the stability of the region. The UWSA today is stronger and much better armed than the old CPB ever was. China may only want to see a UWSA that has enough weapons to deter the Burmese government's forces from launching an attack—but war is also a possibility.

That would have disastrous consequences for a small nation that already has suffered badly from decades of fighting, first against the government, then against Khun Sa's army, and more recently against the Shan State Army-South. *Time* reported in its December 16, 2002, cover story on the Golden Triangle drug trade that war has killed one in four Wa men in recent decades. According to Hideyuki Takano, a Japanese writer who spent six months in 1996 with the Was, "These deaths have been devastating for the villages. With so few men around, the social fabric of traditional Wa life is unraveling."

In order to maintain the strength of its forces, the UWSA has recruited children into its ranks. Human Rights Watch stated in a 2002 report that the UWSA orders every family to give up one son. A recent deserter from the UWSA told Human Rights Watch that 10 percent of the boys in his camp were under eighteen and 3 to 4 percent under fifteen. A 2007 report from Human Rights Watch stated that the UWSA "conduct sweeps on villages in which they take boys as young as twelve."

And it is not only Thailand and other neighboring countries that have been affected by the surge in the production of *yaba* from Wei Xuegang's laboratories. Burma, too, has a growing drug problem. The actual number of addicts is not known, but a 2006 report from a Burmese government agency stated that "ATS (amphetamine-type stimulants) users are generally in the age range from twenty to forty years," while Kengtung in Shan State and Kawthaung in the far south had the youngest average age at seventeen and nineteen years respectively. Mandalay had the oldest average for ATS use at forty-two years. But everywhere, most users were found among high school students, out-of-school youths, and highway drivers.

The misery is likely to continue as long as there is no solution to Burma's ethnic crisis, and it is not likely to be solved by changing the name of the country to Myanmar. Most Was would not even consider themselves citizens of Burma: as the Wa representatives had said at the Frontier Areas Commission of Enquiry in the late 1940s, "In the past we have been very independent." No central government in Burma has ever controlled the Wa Hills. During the British time there were the annual flag marches up to the Chinese border, but little else. After independence, the Wa Hills were occupied by nationalist Chinese Kuomintang forces or controlled by local warlords. Then the area came under the rule of the CPB, and since the 1989 mutiny it has been a "special region" administered by the UWSA with minimal Burmese government presence.

Somewhat ironically, the UWSA- and NDAA-controlled areas in Burma may be the freest in a country that has been stifled by decades of military rule. There are few restrictions on normal trade, and e-mail and the Internet are not controlled or censored by the authorities. Those who can afford to do so can buy and use mobile phones—but it is all via Chinese providers, not Burmese ones.

It will not be an easy task for any government to integrate the Wa Hills with the rest of the country. The Was would never accept a unitary state in which they are classified as "Myanmars," no different from the Burmese and other nationalities in the country. The same could be said of the Shans, who have been fighting for autonomy since 1958—and are still fighting. The Karens have been fighting since 1949, and have never forgotten the tactical mistakes of the Burmese nationalists during the Japanese occupation. Unlike the Shans, who signed the Panglong agreement and trusted Aung San, the Karens did not take part in any negotiations with the central authorities before or after Burma's independence.

It should be clear that no regional or international anti-drug policy has any chance of success unless it is linked to a lasting solution to Burma's ethnic issues and to the establishment of a meaningful democratic process in the country—unless there is no interest in stemming the flow of first heroin and then methamphetamines into Thailand and beyond. But the UN and the world have kept ignoring these fundamental issues, and that is part of the problem, not the solution.

Global Hypocrisy and a New Approach?

The West likes to posture itself as a champion in the "war on drugs"— but in Asia it is not forgotten that opium brought in by Western traders enslaved millions of people in China and elsewhere during the colonial era. Just in time for Hong Kong's return to China on July 1, 1997, the Chinese movie industry released a mega production called *The Opium War*, which depicted commissioner Lin Zexu as a national hero and the British as brutal aggressors. In more recent times the United States supported the Kuomintang, which built up the Golden Triangle opium trade. The nationalist Chinese were allies in the war against the perceived threats of communism, so a blind eye was turned to the means through which they financed their struggle.

Panghsang and Möng La may have been built on income from the drug trade—but so were Hong Kong, Calcutta, Madras, Bombay, and Saigon. It may be rather far-fetched to expect the world to accept Hong Pang and the Shwe Lin Star Company as respectable, as it has done with Jardine-Matheson and the British East India Company—for we are living in different times, with other values—but it is certainly not without precedent for companies that once were heavily engaged in the drug trade to turn to other, more wholesome activities. Western policymakers must understand that many people in Asia see their narcotics policies as deeply hypocritical.

It is easy to moralize about drugs and blame the problem solely on insurgents and former insurgents, but even the Rangoon-based United Nations drug researcher Xavier Bouan conceded in October 2007 that all armies in the area, including the government's, "are taxing this crop." In other words, the situation is not that different than it was in the mid-nineteenth century, when the American merchant W.C. Hunter declared:

"We were all equally implicated." There are no angels *or* devils in the Golden Triangle; they are often one and the same.

It may be a flawed approach to ask whether the UWSA is a narco-army or an ethnic nationalist movement, as Dutch researcher Tom Kramer does in his work on the Was, but demonizing them because of their involvement in the drug trade is not going to lead to any kind of solution to the problem either. In fact, doing so can be considered counterproductive. Engaging them may be the only way forward, and it is possible that the world missed a potentially significant opportunity when it dismissed Saw Lu's proposals in 1993 and insisted on working only through the UN and "recognized governments."

That was actually not the first time that a group involved in the drug trade had made such an appeal to the international community. In 1973, when Lo Hsing-han had refused to disband his home guard unit and gone underground to link up with the then undivided Shan State Army (SSA), the Shans persuaded him to submit a proposal to the US government to terminate the opium trade. The proposal included a clause saying that the SSA and its allies "will invite observers from the United States Narcotics Bureau, or any similar body to visit the opium areas of Shan State and to submit information about opium convoys on their own wireless transmitters." But Lo Hsing-han was arrested and the proposal rejected.

In 1975, also, the SSA persuaded Khun Sa's chief of staff, Sao Hpalang, to sign and submit a similar proposal to the US government. Two years later, after Khun Sa had been freed from jail in Burma, US congressman Lester Wolff sent Joseph Nellis, chief counsel of the Select Committee on Narcotics Abuse and Control, to Ban Hin Taek, where he held talks with the drug lord. However, the US State Department once more declined any cooperation with the groups in Shan State: "The narcotics trade has long fostered a state of lawlessness over wide areas of Burma and northern Thailand. The rule of law in those areas has been replaced by the depredations of warlord armies and bandits such as Chan Shee-fu's (Zhang Qifu, or Khun Sa) so-called Shan United Army. We, therefore, stressed the need for law enforcement."

The US government provided the Burmese with helicopters and fixed-wing aircraft that were supposed to be used to interdict opium convoys. In reality, they were deployed in ordinary counterinsurgency operations. Ten years later, the US General Accounting Office concluded that "enforcement efforts in Burma are not effective." US assistance had not reduced opium production and the State Department had not collected "adequate data to determine if resources were used appropriately and if they contributed to anti-narcotics objectives." In fact, those efforts may not only have been ineffective but also counterproductive, as all they may have done is push the leadership of the Was and other ethnic minorities in Burma into a corner where they have no choice but to continue their reliance on the drug trade and alliance with narco-profiteers like Wei Xuegang, who have neither the fundamental interest of the Wa at heart nor the UWSA's broader political ambitions of creating an autonomous homeland for the Wa people.

US assistance to Burma's "anti-drug efforts" was cut off in the wake of the massacres in 1988, and Washington has since then been much more critical of the Burmese generals and their pledges to fight narcotics, a position that was reflected in official statements made when Asia World was sanctioned in early 2008. But the US has not offered any alternative course of action, and continues to insist on an intensified law enforcement campaign, as with the 2005 indictments of the UWSA leaders.

It would not be realistic to expect anyone to negotiate with Wei Xuegang—and, huddled down in his bunker at Nalawt, he does not seem to be interested in communicating with the outside world either. But as the arrest and release of the field commander Ta Htang shows, the UWSA is not a monolithic organization. Bao Youxiang may not be the ideal leader, and many of his initiatives for the "development" of the area under his control are certainly ill-conceived, but the Wa have nobody else who can speak for them, and he does generally command the respect of his people.

But to stress the obvious, any discussions with him or other Wa leaders would have to go beyond both law enforcement issues and UNODC-style "development programs." They would have to include talks about the future status of the Wa Hills and other minority areas—and there, of course, the present government of Burma would not be willing to make any political concessions that would jeopardize its vision of a unitary State of Myanmar. So, in the final analysis, Burma would have to become democratic and adopt some kind of federal system that recognizes the aspirations of the country's many ethnic minorities before the world can expect any real progress in the fight against drugs.

The National League for Democracy (NLD), which was founded by Aung San's daughter Aung San Suu Kyi after the 1988 uprising—and which won a landslide victory in a general election in 1990 but was never allowed to form a government—made this point as early as in 1989:

> The forty-year history of [ethnic] relations has been a chapter of misfortune verging on the tragic. Along Burma's extended borders from the extreme north to the far south there are no less than thirteen groups of insurgents—a situation which is sapping the strength and resources of the nation. The development of the country has suffered greatly since approximately 40 percent of the national budget has to be devoted to defense requirements. For these reasons we must seek a lasting solution to the problems of the ethnic minorities . . . it is the aim of the League to secure the highest degree of autonomy consonant with the inherent rights of the minorities and the well-being of the Union as a whole.

The NLD today may be a pale shadow of what it was in 1989 and 1990, having been cowed into submission by the country's military rulers and having had most of its leaders imprisoned or put under house arrest—like Aung San Suu Kyi herself. But the policy they outlined almost twenty years ago is still valid, and crucial, even though there has since been ceasefire agreements and reduced fighting in the border areas.

The refusal to accept the realities of Burma's ethnic conflict, or the attempt to bury them under the cloak of "Myanmar" and hide from the public in an isolated hill resort in Maymyo, will only prolong the misery that keeps the people in virtual slavery—and keeps the drugs flowing out of the country in all directions. There should be no doubt that the future stability of the entire region depends on a solution to Burma's decades-long ethnic conflict. That issue is not just Burma's own "internal affair" but a problem that affects everyone—from *yaba* addicts to the victims of their crazed habit; from governments struggling to come to terms with corruption to financial institutions tarnished by the flow of black money. No one is left untouched by the wiles of these merchants of madness.

LIST OF ACRONYMS

ATS	Amphetamine-type stimulants
BSPP	Burma Socialist Program Party
CPB	Communist Party of Burma
DEA	Drug Enforcement Administration
DKBA	Democratic Karen Buddhist Army
KIO/KIA	Kachin Independence Organization/Army
KDA	Kachin Democratic Army (sometimes referred to as the Kachin Defense Army)
KNLA	Karen National Liberation Army
KNU	Karen National Union
MDMA	Methylenedioxymethamphetamine (ecstasy)
MNDAA	Myanmar National Democratic Alliance Army
MTA	Möng Tai Army
NDA	New Democratic Army
NDAA (ESS)	National Democratic Alliance Army (Eastern Shan State)
NLD	National League for Democracy
ONCB	Office of Narcotics Control Board
SLORC	State Law and Order Restoration Council
SPDC	State Peace and Development Council
SSA	Shan State Army
SSRC	Shan State Restoration Council
SUA	Shan United Army
SURA	Shan United Revolutionary Army
UNDCP	United Nations Drug Control Program
UNFDAC	United Nations Fund for Drug Abuse Control
UNODC	United Nations Office on Drugs and Crime
UWSP/UWSA	United Wa State Party/Army
WNC	Wa National Council
WNO/WNA	Wa National Organization/Army

WHO'S WHO
IN THE GOLDEN TRIANGLE

Bang Ron (Surachai Ngernthongfoo)
Sino-Thai drug kingpin. Allegedly leader of one of Thailand's largest amphetamine distribution networks until the Thai police raided his home in Kanchanaburi province in October 1998. Managed to escape to Burma, where he linked up with the drug lord Wei Xuegang (q.v.) and the United Wa State Army. Now believed to be moving between Laos and the UWSA-controlled areas of northeastern Shan State. Number four on Thailand's ten-most-wanted list.

Bao Youxiang (Bao Yuchang; Ta Pang)
Wa. Born in 1949 in the Hkwin Ma area of the northern Wa Hills. Local warlord who began receiving support from the Communist Party of Burma in October 1969. Commander (with Li Ziru as the political commissar) of the CPB's 683 Brigade, which was active in central Shan State until the 1989 mutiny. Became an alternate member of the CPB's central committee at the third congress in 1985. Following the collapse of the CPB, he became military commander of the United Wa State Army and also chairman of the United Wa State Party when in 1995 Chao Ngi Lai (q.v.) suffered a stroke. His elder brother Bao Youri works for Wei Xuegang (q.v.) while his younger brother Bao Youliang commands Möng Mao in the northern Wa Hills. The youngest of the Bao brothers, Bao Youhua, died of a massive stroke on August 26, 2007. He was known to be a heavy drinker, a drug user, and a womanizer.

Chao Ngi Lai (Zhao Yilai; Kyauk Nyi Laing; Ta Lai)
Wa. Born in 1939 in Kyauk Chung village, northern Wa Hills. Local warlord in the Saohin-Saohpa area, northern Wa Hills. Contacted by the Communist Party of Burma in 1968; captured Saohpa together with regular CPB

forces in December 1969. Appointed battalion commander in the CPB's army and became an alternate member of the central committee at the third congress in 1985. One of the most important leaders of the March–April 1989 mutiny; elected general secretary of the new Burma National United Party in May 1989 and leader of its successor, the United Wa State Party, on November 3, 1989. The party was legalized shortly afterwards and its armed wing, the United Wa State Army, was recognized by the Burmese government as a local militia force. Suffered a stroke in 1995 and is now inactive.

Ho Chung (Hsiao Ho; Haw Zengtien)

Wa. Born in Dehong prefecture of China's Yunnan province. Bao Youxiang's (q.v.) son-in-law, married to his daughter Bao Yina. Handles money-laundering operations for Bao and Wei Xuegang. A frequent visitor to the annual gems auction in Rangoon and considered close to Burmese military intelligence operatives, with whom he often plays golf.

Li Ziru

Chinese. Born in 1946 in Baoshan in China's Yunnan province. Joined the Communist Party of Burma as a Red Guard-volunteer in 1968. Political commissar attached to the CPB's 683 Brigade, which was commanded by Bao Youxiang (q.v.). Became an alternate member of the central committee during the CPB's third congress in 1985. Joined the 1989 mutiny and became one of the leaders of the Panghsang-based Burma National Unity Party, renamed the United Wa State Party on November 3, 1989. Appointed deputy commander-in-chief and chief-of-staff of the United Wa State Army in 1989. Passed away on January 5, 2005, and his part of the Wa business empire is run now by his sons Li Zuhua and Lin Ching. They maintain a "headquarters within the headquarters" at Wan Nalawt, west of Panghsang.

Lin Mingxian (Sai Leün; U Sai Lin)

Sino-Shan. Comes from Panghsai on the Chinese border in northern Shan State. Member of a Red Guard–style organization in Yunnan during the Cultural Revolution. Joined the Communist Party of Burma in 1968 as a volunteer together with Zhang Zhiming, Li Ziru (q.v.), and other Chinese Red Guards. One of the CPB's ablest field commanders; in charge of the 815 War Zone (Eastern Shan State). Married the daughter of Kokang chieftain Peng Jiasheng's (q.v.). Joined the 1989 mutiny and is now militia commander close to the Burmese government. His militia is called the National Democratic Alliance Army (Eastern Shan State) and controls the area along the Yunnan frontier from Möng La to the Mekong river. He has invested heavily in casinos in northern Burma and, more recently, at Boten on Laos's border with China. Now one of the wealthiest operators in the Golden Triangle.

Lo Hsing-han (Luo Xinghan)

Kokang Chinese. Born in 1934 in Ta Tsu Chin village, Kokang. Joined the local Kokang Army of the ruling Yang family in the early 1960s. Defected to the Burmese government in 1963 and was appointed commander of the Kokang Ka Kwe Ye home guards. One of the KKY commanders who benefited the most from the opium deal with Rangoon, and emerged as a prominent drug trafficker in the early 1970s. Went underground when Rangoon disbanded the KKY in 1973, then teamed up with the Shan State Army. In August 1973 crossed the border to Thailand, where he was arrested and extradited to Rangoon. Sentenced to death for "rebellion against the state" in 1976. Pardoned during a general amnesty in 1980. Acted as go-between for Rangoon to negotiate with Communist Party of Burma mutineers in 1989. Now back in business together with Peng Jiasheng, Peng Jiafu, and other former CPB commanders who have since become government-recognized militia commanders. Lo's business empire, which includes the conglomerate Asia World, is now run by his son, Steven Law aka Tun Myint Naing. In February 2008 the United States sanctioned companies owned by the Lo family for their support for Burma's military government.

Mahasang

Wa. Born in 1946 in Kwan Mau village near Vingngun in the Wa Hills. The second son of Sao Maha, *aka* Ta Hpawng, the last *saohpa* (prince) of Vingngun. Commander of Vingngun Ka Kwe Ye in the late 1960s to early 1970s. Driven out of the area by the communists in 1972. Went underground with

Lo Hsing-han (Luo Xinghan) in 1973 and came down with him to the Thai border. First allied with the Shan State Army, which helped him set up the Wa State Army in 1974. Broke with the SSA in 1977 and joined forces with Kuomintang and Moh Heing's Shan United Revolutionary Army. The political wing of the WNA, the Wa National Organization, joined the National Democratic Front in 1983. Mahasang was sent by the NDF to negotiate with the CPB mutineers in May–June 1989; was arrested by them but managed to escape and reached Thailand a few months later. In November 1989 the Wa National Council, officially the administrative arm of the WNO but in reality a separate organization led by Ai Kyaw Hsö, merged with the Wa units of the former CPB and the combined force became the United Wa State Army. Mahasang was arrested in March 2005 during a drug-sting operation that went wrong. Died in December 2007 in a hospital near the main prison in the northern Thai city of Chiang Mai. Mahasang's younger brother Mahaja joined the Möng Tai Army and became an influential local militia commander in southern Shan State after Khun Sa's surrender in January 1996.

Naw Kham
Ethnic Shan leader of a Lahu militia. Born around 1960 and a native of the Tachilek area of eastern Shan State. Previously a supply officer for Khun Sa's Möng Tai Army living in Mae Sai across the border in Thailand. Became a local militia leader and prominent drug trafficker following Khun Sa's surrender on January 7, 1996. Went underground when, on January 9, 2006, his home in Tachilek was raided by Burmese authorities, probably at the insistence of China's security agencies. Now operates along the Mekong river where it forms the border between Burma and Laos. A close associate of Lahu warlord Yishe (q.v.).

Peng Jiasheng (Pheung Kya-shin)
Kokang Chinese. Born in 1931 in Hong Seu Htoo village, Kokang. Officer in the Kokang Revolutionary Force, which was set up by the ruling Yang family in the 1960s. Contacted by Communist Party of Burma cadres in China in July 1967 and promised arms and ammunition. Went to Beijing with his younger brother Peng Jiafu shortly afterwards. Entered Kokang from China on January 5, 1968, as commander of the Kokang People's

Liberation Army, which officially merged with the CPB in August of the same year. Led civil administration in Kokang although he never joined the party. Entered the heroin trade in the early 1970s. Initiated the mutiny in March 1989 together with Peng Jiafu. Became a government-recognized militia commander and one of Burma's most prominent drug traffickers. Lost out to the Yang clan in late 1992, and was forced to flee Kokang. In recent years, the Pengs and the Yangs have reconciled, but factionalism and infighting continue among the former CPB forces in Kokang and Möng Ko west of the Salween.

Saw Lu (Saul; Ta Pluik)
Wa. Born in 1942 in Kengtung. Studied at Dr. Gordon Seagrave's missionary school in Namkham and later at the Karen Baptist School in Myaungmya. Became a Ka Kwe Ye home guard commander in Saohpa (Pangwei) in the Wa Hills in 1964. Driven out by the communists in 1969. Later a high-ranking official in the ruling Burma Socialist Program Party. Helped set up the Wa National Development Party and the Lahu National Development Party (his wife Mary is a Lahu) in 1988. Arrested by the military authorities in Lashio on January 21, 1992, and charged with "cooperating with the CIA and the DEA." Released after pressure from Wa commander Chao Ngi Lai (who had captured Saohpa in 1969) on March 16, 1992. Joined the United Wa State Party in April and served as its chief international liaison officer until he was ousted in 1995.

Wei Hsaitang (Ta Htang)
Wa. Born in the early 1950s. No relation to Wei Xuegang (q.v.). Well-known combat commander of the United Wa State Army and was active along the Thai border fighting the Shan State Army-South throughout the 1990s. Later fell out with the Panghsang leadership, which had him arrested in 2002. He spent five years behind bars before being rehabilitated in May 2007. Not attached to the UWSA's military headquarters in Panghsang.

Wei Xuegang (Wei Hsueh-kang; Prasit [Charnchai] Chiwinitipanya; U Sein Win; Somboon Kadumporn)
Chinese, from Yunnan. Born in 1952 according to his now-revoked Thai

ID card, but in reality several years before. Fled with his family to the Wa Hills following the communist takeover in China. Based for many years in Vingngun in the Wa Hills together with his elder brother Wei Xuelong (Wei Hsueh-long aka Apichart Chiwinprapasri) and younger brother Wei Xueyin (Wei Hseuh-yin aka Pairot Sameur Jayneuk). The three Wei brothers were connected with the Kuomintang-CIA spy network along the Yunnan frontier until the Burmese Communists drove them out in the early 1970s. Wei first joined Khun Sa's (Zhang Qifu's) forces on the Thai border, and he served for several years as the drug lord's treasurer. During that time he traveled extensively to West Germany, Taiwan, and many other countries. Later, he fell out with Khun Sa and was imprisoned near his base at Ban Hin Taek, near the Burmese border in northern Thailand. But he managed to escape and took refuge in Taiwan from 1982 to 1983. He then returned to the Thai-Burma border areas where he established his own heroin empire. Lacking an army inside Burma, the Wei brothers made use of their old Wa contacts and bankrolled the buildup of the Wa National Army in the early 1980s. They joined the United Wa State Party in 1989, and Wei Xuegang served as UWSA/P financial affairs chief from July 4, 2006, to late December 2007, when he was succeeded by his deputy Bao Youliang but remains the most powerful financial controller of the Wa movement. He now lives in a luxurious mansion near Panghsang. His elder brother, Wei Xuelong, is living in retirement in the UWSA-controlled area, while the younger brother, Wei Xueyin, remains affiliated with major UWSA-controlled business enterprises.

Xiao Minliang (Xiao Min Liang)
Vice-chairman of the United Wa State Party and a main spokesman for the organization. Lives in Panghsang, where he often receives UN officials and other foreign visitors. Considered a figurehead for Wei Xuegang.

Yang Molian (Yang Mo Lian)
Kokang Chinese. Born in 1951 in Kokang, where he attended primary school. Joined the Kokang army in 1966 and, in 1968, the forces of the Communist Party of Burma. Military officer in the CPB's army until the 1989 mutiny. Defeated Peng Jiasheng in the 1992 "opium war" in Kokang,

but the two clans have since reconciled. Yang's younger brother Yang Muxian was executed in Kunming on October 7, 1994, for trafficking in heroin in China.

Yawt Serk (Yawt Suk; Yawt Seik)
Shan. Born in 1959 in Möng Nawng near Loilem, Shan State. Joined the Shan resistance in 1976, first as radio operator for Moh Heing's Shan United Revolutionary Army and then as combat officer in the Möng Tai Army after Moh Heing merged his SURA (then renamed Tai-land Revolutionary Army) with Khun Sa's Shan United Army on March 25, 1985. Refused to surrender when, in January 1996, Khun Sa negotiated a deal with the Burmese government. Resurrected the Shan United Revolutionary Army, which assumed the name Shan State Army on January 1, 1998. His group is usually referred to as Shan State Army-South to distinguish it from the Shan State Army-North, which has a cease-fire agreement with the Burmese government.

Yishe (Chaiwat Pornsakulpaisarn)
Lahu. Son of a respected Baptist preacher in Kengtung, eastern Shan State. Joined Khun Sa's Shan United Army in 1980. Acquired Thai citizenship and surrendered with Khun Sa on January 7, 1996, and became a local militia leader in the Tachilek area of eastern Shan State. His home in the northern Thai city of Chiang Mai was raided by Thai police on December 28, 2003. Now based at Nampong, west of Tachilek.

Zhang Qifu (Chang Shifu; Khun Sa; Chan Changtrakul)
Sino-Shan. Born in 1934 in Hpa-perng village in the Loi Maw area of Möng Yai, northern Shan State, of a Chinese father and a Shan mother. His father died when he was a child and his mother remarried the Shan *myosa* (or tax collector under the Möng Yai *saohpa*) of Möng Tawm. Zhang grew up with his Chinese grandfather, who was the headman of Loi Maw. Joined an armed band in the Loi Maw area in the early 1950s and frequently shifted sides between the government and the rebels. In 1963 his private army was converted into a government-recognized Ka Kwe Ye home guard unit under the northeastern command of the Burmese Army in Lashio. His

men attacked Shan rebel forces and in return he was allowed to trade in opium and heroin. Became one of Burma's most prominent drug traffickers in the 1960s, but lost to Kuomintang rivals in the famous battle at the Lao-Thai-Burmese border junction in July 1967. His fortunes dwindled and he was arrested by the Burmese authorities on October 20, 1969. His men subsequently went underground and on April 16, 1973, kidnapped two Soviet doctors from the hospital in Taunggyi. In exchange for their freedom, Zhang was released from Mandalay jail on September 7, 1974. He joined his men underground in February 1976 and moved to Ban Hin Taek, near the Burmese border in northern Thailand. He then assumed the Shan name Khun Sa and his former home guard unit was renamed the Shan United Army. He was forced out of Thailand in January 1982 but quickly built new bases on the Burmese side of the border, where he established a new working relationship with Burma's military authorities. He merged his SUA with Moh Heing's former Shan United Revolutionary Army on March 25, 1985; the combined forces assumed the name the Möng Tai Army in 1987. He surrendered to the Burmese government on January 7, 1996, disbanded his army and moved to Rangoon with his money. He died in Rangoon on October 26, 2007. Zhang, or Khun Sa, was one of the most colorful and flamboyant of all the warlords of the Golden Triangle, and very well connected in Burma, Thailand, and beyond. Apart from dealing in opium and heroin, he was also instrumental in introducing methamphetamine production to Burma in the early 1990s. The family business—gems, casinos, and reportedly also drugs—is now being run by his sons and daughters, who live in Rangoon and in Tachilek.

Zhang Suquan (Chang Su-chuang; Sao Hpalang)
Chinese. Born in 1927 in Liaoning, Manchuria. Joined the Kuomintang during World War II; based at Chongqing (Chungking) and Whampoa. Fled to Burma following the communist victory in China. Evacuated to Taiwan in 1952. Served briefly as an intelligence officer in Korea. Served with the US-supported Bataillon Spécial 111 in Laos 1960–63. Returned to Shan State in the mid 1960s; Khun Sa's chief of staff and main military strategist until he surrendered to the Burmese government in January 1996. Became a prominent businessman in Rangoon.

Zhang Zhiming (Kyi Myint)

Chinese. Born in 1950 in Wanting, Yunnan. Joined the Communist Party of Burma in 1968 as a Red Guard volunteer along with Li Ziru and Lin Mingxian. One of the CPB's ablest military officers. Commander of the Second Brigade at Möng Paw; in November 1986 led a massive assault on government positions on Hsi-Hsinwan mountain in northern Shan State. Supported the mutiny in April 1989 and joined Lin Mingxian's force in the Möng La area in eastern Shan State in May. Instrumental in transforming Möng La to a booming gambling center, but now keeps a low profile.

ANNOTATED BIBLIOGRAPHY

BOOKS AND INDEPENDENT STUDIES

Chin, Ko-lin, and Sheldon X. Zhang. *The Chinese Connection: Cross-border Trafficking between Myanmar and China*. Washington: US Department of Justice, April 2007. 117 pp. A detailed study of the drug trade along the Sino-Burmese border, including interviews with local law enforcement officials and drug traffickers.

Chouvy, Pierre-Arnaud, and Joel Meissonnier. *Yaba: Production, Traffic and Consumption of Methamphetamine in Mainland Southeast Asia*. Singapore: Singapore University Press, 2004. 210 pp. One of very few books specifically about the production and use of *yaba* in Southeast Asia.

Fiskesjö, Magnus. *The Fate of Sacrifice and the Making of Wa History*. Unpublished Ph.D. Dissertation. Chicago: University of Chicago, 2000 (UMI Number 9959092). 487 pp. The most detailed account of the Wa that has been written in recent years. Available digitally at the University of Hong Kong Libraries.

Jelsma, Martin, and Tom Kramer, Pietje Vervest (eds.). *Trouble in the Triangle: Opium and Conflict in Burma*. Chiang Mai: Silkworm Books, 2005. A collection of essays about ethnicity and drugs in Burma, but of varying standards. Some chapters are informative and comprehensive, but others are of questionable value.

Kramer, Tom. *The United Wa State Party: Narco-Army or Ethnic Nationalist Party?* Policy Studies 38 (Southeast Asia). Washington: East-West Center, 2007. 99 pp. A brief overview of the UWSP and its activities.

Lamour, Catherine, and Michael R. Lamberti. *The Second Opium War*. London: Allen Lane, 1974. 278 pp. About the Golden Triangle opium trade but not up to the standards of McCoy's books.

Lintner, Bertil. *Burma in Revolt: Opium and Insurgency since 1948*. 3rd ed. Chiang Mai: Silkworm Books, 2003. 558 pp. About Burma's decades-long civil war and the intertwined drug problem.

———. *The Rise and Fall of the Communist Party of Burma*. Ithaca, New York: Cornell University Southeast Asia Program, 1990. 124 pp. A history of Burma's Communist movement as well as an account of the 1989 mutiny.

———. "Heroin and Highland Insurgency in the Golden Triangle." In *War on Drugs: Studies in the Failure of US Narcotics Policy*, edited by Alfred M. McCoy and Alan A. Block. Boulder, San Francisco and Oxford: Westview Press, 1992, 281–317.

———. *The Politics of the Drug Trade in Burma*. Indian Ocean Center for Peace Studies, Occasional Paper No. 33. Nedlands: The University of Western Australia, 1993. 63 pp.

———. "Drugs, Insurgency and Counterinsurgency in Burma." In *Burma: Myanmar in the Twenty-First Century, Dynamics of Continuity and Change*, edited by John J. Brandon. Bangkok: Open Society Institute, Thai Studies Section, 1997, 245–97.

———. "Drugs and Economic Growth in Burma Today," in *Burma/Myanmar: Strong Regime Weak State*. Adelaide: Crawford Publishing House, 2000: 164–194.

McCoy, Alfred W. *The Politics of Heroin in Southeast Asia*. New York: Harper & Row, 1972. 472 pp. An outstanding and authoritative account of the narcotics trade in Southeast Asia in the 1970s.

———. *The Politics of Heroin: CIA Complicity in the Global Drug Trade*. New York: Lawrence Hill Books, 1991. 634 pp. A revised and updated version of McCoy's first book.

———. *The Politics of Heroin: CIA Complicity in the Global Drug Trade*. New York: Lawrence Hill Books, 2003. 710 pp. A second revised and updated version of McCoy's first book.

Pasuk Phongpauchit, Sungsidh Piriyarangsan, and Nualnoi Treerat. *Guns, Girls, Gambling, Ganja: Thailand's Illegal Economy and Public Policy*. Chiang Mai: Silkworm Books, 1998. 284 pp. Covers various aspects of Thailand's underground economy, including the drug trade.

Renard, Ronald. *The Burma Connection: Illegal Drugs & the Making of the Golden Triangle*. Boulder and London: Lynne Rienner Publishers, 1996. 147 pp. A comprehensive history of the emergence of the Golden Triangle drug trade.

Smith, Martin. *Burma: Insurgency and the Politics of Ethnicity*. London: Zed Press, 1991. 492 pp. A detailed study of Burma's civil war and its ethnic problems.

Takano, Hideyuki. *The Shore Beyond Good and Evil: A Report from Inside Burma's Opium Kingdom*. Tokyo: Kotan Publishing, 2002. 277 pp. A unique account of life in the Wa Hills of Burma by a Japanese who spent months in the area.

Weil, Andrew, and Winifred Rosen. *From Chocolate to Morphine: Everything You Need to Know About Mind-Altering Drugs.* Boston and New York: Houghton Mifflin Company, 2004. 294 pp. An overview of various kinds of drugs by one of America's best-known doctors.

Zaw Oo and Win Min. *Assessing Burma's Ceasefire Accords.* Policy Studies 39 (Southeast Asia). Washington: East-West Center, 2007. 91 pp. An assessment of the cease-fire agreements between the Burmese government and various rebel armies since 1989.

SELECTED ARTICLES

Asif, Edo (with Anthony Davis). "United Wa State Army Prepares for Confrontation." *Jane's Defence Weekly*, October 18, 2006.

Atiya Achakulwisut. "Driven on Dope." *Bangkok Post*, October 15, 1991.

Black, Michael. "Myanmar Faces Down its Armed Minorities." *Jane's Intelligence Review*, March 2006.

———. "Access Denied: Thai Opium Crop Substitution Program in Burma Hits Problems." *Irrawaddy*, April 2006.

——— (with Roland Fields). "The Real 'Long War' is in Myanmar." *Asia Times Online*, June 10, 2006.

——— (with Roland Fields). "On Patrol with the Shan State Army." *Irrawaddy*, July 2006.

——— (with Roland Fields). "Virtual Gambling in Myanmar's Drug Country." *Asia Times Online*, August 26, 2006.

———. "Myanmar's Largest Drug Militia at Crossroads." *Asia Times Online*, October 24, 2006.

———. "Sino-Myanmar Co-operation Forces Wa to Rethink." *Jane's Terrorism and Security Monitor*, November 15, 2006.

———. "On Myanmar-China Border, Tensions Escalate Between SPDC, Narco-Militias." *World Politics Watch*, December 13, 2006.

———. "Wei Xueh-gang: The UWSA's Narcotics Kingpin." *Jane's Terrorism and Security Monitor*, March 14, 2007.

——— (with Anthony Davis). "Wa and Peace—The UWSA and Tensions in Myanmar." *Jane's Intelligence Review*, March 2008.

—— (with Anthony Davis). "Drug traffickers target Vietnam." *Jane's Intelligence Digest*, June 6, 2008.

Cabrera, Jaime, and Chitraporn Vanaspong. "Confessions of a Young *Yaba* Addict." *Bangkok Post*, March 16, 1997.

Davis, Anthony (with Bruce Hawke). "Burma: the Country that Won't Kick the Habit." *Jane's Intelligence Review*, March 1998.

——. "Southeast Asian Crime Syndicates Turn to 'Ice.'" *Jane's Intelligence Review*, September 2006.

Hawke, Bruce. "Burma's Ceasefire Agreements in Danger of Unraveling." *Jane's Intelligence Review*, November 1998.

Lintner, Bertil. "The Shans and the Shan State of Burma." *Contemporary Southeast Asia* 5, no. 4 (March 1984).

——. "Smack in the Face." *Far Eastern Economic Review*, November 5, 1992. New ex-CPB narcotics chieftains usurp traditional drug barons.

——. "Tracing New Tracks." *Far Eastern Economic Review*, March 18, 1993. Ex-CPB warlords smuggle drugs to Laos and Cambodia.

——. "A Fatal Overdose/Chinese Takeaway." *Far Eastern Economic Review*, June 3, 1993. New drug routes from the Golden Triangle.

——. "Khun Sa: Asia's Drug King on the Run." *Far Eastern Economic Review*, January 20, 1994. Cover story on Rangoon's offensive against Khun Sa, including an interview with the drug lord.

——. "Divide and Rule." *Far Eastern Economic Review*, January 27, 1994. Peace treaties with ethnic rebel armies marginalize democracy groups.

——. "Plague without Borders." *Far Eastern Economic Review*, July 21, 1994. Drug-and-AIDS culture spreads across region.

——. "Golden Triangle Handshake." *Far Eastern Economic Review*, January 25, 1996. Khun Sa surrenders, but on his own terms.

——. "A Drug Lord Surrenders." *Tokyo Journal*, March 1996. The surrender of Khun Sa.

——. "A Blind Eye to Drugs." *Far Eastern Economic Review*, November 7, 1996. The role of drug money in the Burmese economy.

——. "Narcopolitics in Burma." *Current History*, December 1996.

——. "Speed Demons." *Far Eastern Economic Review*, May 8, 1997. Asia's newest drug scourge: mass-produced stimulants.

————. "Safe at Home." *Far Eastern Economic Review*, August 14, 1997. Burmese drug lords are keeping their cash in the country.

————. "Drug Tide Strain Ties/Australia Counts Cost." *Far Eastern Economic Review*, September 9, 1999.

———— (with Rodney Tasker). "Danger: Road Works Ahead." *Far Eastern Economic Review*, December 21, 2000.

———— (with Rodney Tasker). "Nasty Job for Task Force 399." *Far Eastern Economic Review*, April 19, 2001.

————. "Drugs and Politics." *Far Eastern Economic Review*, February 7, 2002.

————. "Myanmar Drugs Fuel Thai Gangs." *Asia Times Online*, October 23, 2007.

————. "UN Fiddles While Myanmar Burns." *Asia Times Online*, October 23, 2007.

————. "Death of a Drug Lord." *Asia Times Online*, November 1, 2007.

McCartan, Brian. "A Big Time Business Drug Trafficker's Singaporean Connection." *Asia Sentinel*, February 29, 2008.

Marshall, Andrew (with Anthony Davis). "Speed Tribe/Soldiers of Fortune." *Time* (Asia), December 16, 2002.

Nipada Kheo-Urai. "Pills That Become Killers." *Bangkok Post*, April 8, 1990.

Supradit Kanwanich, Prasong Charasdamrong, and Surat Jinakul. "New Amphetamine Epidemic." *Bangkok Post*, March 16, 1997.

Suvicha Pouaree. "Madness Pills Abuse on the Rise." *Bangkok Post*, October 20, 1996.

Wechsler, Maximilian. "Dangerous Duo/Why Wei Remains Untouchable/The Hong Pang Group." *Bangkok Post*, July 6, 2008.

REPORTS

Amphetamine-Type Stimulants: A Global Review. 139 pp. Prepared by the United Nations International Drug Control Program, Vienna, 1996.

Hand in Glove: the Burma Army and the Drug Trade in Shan State. 64 pp. Published by the Shan Herald Agency for News (SHAN), August 2005. Outlines official Burmese government complicity in the Golden Triangle drug trade.

My Gun Was as Tall as Me: Child Soldiers in Burma. Human Rights Watch, October 2002. 213 pp.

Opium Poppy Cultivation in Southeast Asia: Lao PDR, Myanmar, Thailand. United Nations Office on Drugs and Crime, October 2007. 134 pp. The report completely ignores the methamphetamine problem, because it is not part of the UNODC's mandate in Burma.

Shan Drug Watch/Newsletter, June 2007. A publication of the Shan Herald Agency for News (SHAN)

Show Business: Rangoon's "War on Drugs" in Shan State. 104 pp. Published by the Shan Herald Agency for News (SHAN), April 2005. Exposes as a charade the Burmese military regime's "War on Drugs" in the Golden Triangle.

Sold to be Soldiers: The Recruitment and Use of Child Soldiers in Burma. Human Rights Watch, October 2007.147 pp.

The 2008 International Narcotics Strategy Report (INCRS), Volume 1: Drug and Chemical Control and Volume 2: Money Laundering and Financial Crimes. United States Department of State, May 24, 2008. An annual report by the Department of State to the US Congress. It describes the efforts of key countries to attack all aspects of the international drug trade.

Undercurrents. A report on "blasting the Mekong" river and "turning illegal drug profits into legal revenues" by the Lahu National Development Organization, January 2005. 21 pp.

NOTES ON SOURCES

CHAPTER ONE

The picture of Paitoon Puthiporn and Patcharaphant Jiravanich appeared in several Thai newspapers in August 2002. The quote from Somsak Prisananathakul appeared in the *Bangkok Post* of July 19, 1996, and Preecha Champarat's statement in the *Bangkok Post* of September 12, 1996. The quote from Watcharapol Prasarnrajkit appeared in Pierre-Arnaud Chouvy and Joël Meissonnier, *Yaba: Production, Traffic and Consumption of Methamphetamine in Mainland Southeast Asia* (Singapore: Singapore University Press, 2004), 31–32. Lieutenant General Noppadol Soomboonsap was interviewed in the *Bangkok Post*, March 16, 1997. The interviews with *yaba* users in Chiang Mai were conducted in May 2008, and statistics for drug-related arrests come from *Thailand: Country Summary* (ASEAN and China Cooperative Operations in Response to Dangerous Drugs, November 15, 2006). The statement by Sorasit Sangprasert appeared in the *Bangkok Post* of March 16, 1997 ("New Amphetamine Epidemic," by Supradit Kanwanich, Prasong Charasdamrong, and Surat Jinakul). The list of seizures of *yaba* pills is compiled from reports from Thailand's Office of Narcotics Control Board. Bertil Lintner interviewed Laddawan Chaininpun for an article that appeared in *Asia Times Online* on October 23, 2007 ("Myanmar Drugs Fuel Thai Gangs"). The article also describes the youth gangs of Chiang Mai. The Human Rights Watch report can be found at http://www.hrw.org/campaigns/aids/2004/thai.htm. Maryam Dabhoiwala's article is at http://www.article2.org/mainfile.php/0203/84/. Details about seizures after the 2003 war on drugs come from Anthony Davis, "Southeast Asian Crime Syndicates Turn to 'Ice,'" *Jane's Intelligence Review*, September 2006. The quote from the *Bangkok Post* about increased smuggling in the north was in the June 15, 2008, issue. The background to amphetamine and methamphetamine comes from the online encyclopedia Wikipedia and *Drugs of Abuse*, a booklet compiled by the US Drug Enforcement Administration (Washington DC, 1996.) References to Andrew Weil's findings come from his book *From Chocolate to Morphine: Everything You Need to Know About Mind-Altering Drugs* (Boston and New York: Houghton Mifflin Company, 2004), 53–54. The background to amphetamine and methamphetamine abuse in Thailand is based on an undated paper titled "History of ATS Abuse in Thailand," which was produced by Thai government agencies. The *Bangkok Post* reported on the Ramathibodi Hospital on October 15, 1991 ("Driven on Dope," by Atiya Achakulwisut). The quote from Joël Meissonnier is from *Yaba: Production, Traffic and Consumption*, 85. Details about the situation in Mae Sot and Ranong are from the same book, 61–62. One of the authors of this book went to the tsunami-hit areas in December 2004, and January to February 2005. Supatra Chompoosri's decision to have her son murdered was reported in the *Bangkok Post* of February 4, 1999. Antonio Maria Costa made the statement about the end to poppy production in the Golden Triangle at Doi Tung on February 27, 2006. The quote from Yiu Kong Chu comes from his book *The Triads as Business* (London and New York: Routledge, 2000), viii. The quote from Alfred W. McCoy and Alan A. Block was found in a book they edited, *War on Drugs: Studies in the Failure of US Narcotics Policy* (Boulder, San Francisco & Oxford: Westview Press, 1992), 11.

CHAPTER TWO

For a detailed account of the collapse of the Communist Party of Burma, see Bertil Lintner, *The Rise and Fall of the Communist Party of Burma* (Ithaca, New York: Cornell University Southeast Asia Program, 1990). Notes from the February 20, 1989, meeting in Panghsang was passed on to one of authors during a trip to southern Yunnan in May 1989. Translations of the April 18 and 28, 1989, broadcasts come from SWB, FE/0439B/1, April 20, 1989, and FBIS-EAS-89-081, April 28, 1989, respectively. Details about the rise and fall of the communist movement in Burma come from the authors' notes and are based on interviews with ex-CPB cadres and other sources on the Sino-Burmese border. For a background to the Ka Kwe Ye home guards, see Alfred McCoy, *The Politics of Heroin in Southeast Asia* (New York: Harper & Row, 1972), 314–338, and Bertil Lintner, *Burma in Revolt: Opium and Insurgency since 1948*, 3rd ed. (Chiang Mai: Silkworm Books, 2003), 231–3, 262–4. Figures for Burma's annual opium production come from the US State Department's annual International Narcotics Control Strategy Reports, published by the Bureau of International Narcotics Matters. The description of

Panghsang today is based on personal observations from the time it was under Communist Party of Burma (CPB) control, and after the 1989 mutiny. Statistics about drug addiction in China are from official Chinese sources. See also http://en.wikipedia.org/wiki/Illegal_drug_trade_in_China.

CHAPTER THREE

Alfred McCoy, *The Politics of Heroin in Southeast Asia* (New York: Harper & Row, 1972) gives a comprehensive background to the opium trade in Asia and the Opium Wars with China. See also J.M. Scott, *The White Poppy: A History of Opium* (New York: Funk & Wagnalls, 1969), and Martin Booth, *Opium: A History* (London: Simon & Schuster, 1996). The quote from W.C. Hunter comes from Scott, *The White Poppy*, 84–85. The quote from commissioner Lin Zexu can be found in Samuel M. Wilson, "Coffee, Tea, or Opium?" *Natural History* 11/93: 78. The 1909 British government report that is quoted was published in *The Burma Gazetteer: The Bhamo District* (Rangoon: Superintendent, Central Press, reprinted 1960), 82. Touby Ly Fong is quoted in Catherine Lamour and Michael R. Lamberti, *The Second Opium War* (London: Allen Lane, 1974), 116. The two Shan states of Kengtung and Möng Pan were returned to the British after the war, and their respective princes were reinstated. For a full text of the Panglong Agreement, see Bertil Lintner, "The Shans and the Shan States of Burma," *Contemporary Southeast Asia* 5, no. 4 (Singapore: March 1984). See also Chao Tzang Yawnghwe, *The Shan of Burma: Memoirs of a Shan Exile* (Singapore: Institute of Southeast Asian Studies, 1987). The hearings with the Wa chieftains were published in *Frontier Areas Committee of Enquiry, Part II Appendices* (Rangoon: Superintendent, Government Printing and Stationery, 1947), 37–39. The story about the Sikh doctor who had to be rushed out of the headhunting area is in Sao Saimong Mangrai, *The Shan States and the British Annexation* (Ithaca, New York: Cornell University Southeast Asia Program, Data Paper no. 57, 1965), 271. For an account of the Kuomintang invasion of Burma, see McCoy, *Politics of Heroin*, 126–144, and Bertil Lintner, *Burma in Revolt: Opium and Insurgency Since 1948*, 3rd ed. (Chiang Mai: Silkworm Books, 2003, 125–162. See also *The Kuomintang Aggression Against Burma* (Rangoon: Ministry of Information, 1953. The quote from Duan Xiwen originated in an interview with *The Weekend Telegraph* (London) on March 10,

1967. The quote from Elaine T. Lewis comes from "The Hill Peoples of Kengtung State," *Practical Anthropology* 4, no. 6 (November–December 1957). The quote from Chao Tzang Yawnghwe about the "fast rolling opium bandwagon" comes from "Politics of Burma and Shan State," *Political Science Review* (Chiang Mai University, September 1982). Information about Khun Sa comes from two personal interviews with the warlord in 1993 and 1994. Other details are from Thai and US narcotics intelligence reports. Descriptions of Möng La and Panghsang are based on personal observations at those two towns, when they were under CPB control as well as after the transformation following the 1989 mutiny. Details about the "incense factory" at Panhsang also come from personal observations and informed sources on the ground. See also *Shan Drug Watch Newsletter* (Shan Herald Agency for News, June 2007): 8.

Chapter Four

Details about the Wei brothers can be found in Michael Black, "Wei Xue-gang: The UWSA's Narcotics Kingpin," *Jane's Terrorism & Security Monitor*, March 14, 2007. Other information comes from personal observations in Panghsang and Nalawt, as well as Thai intelligence reports. See also "Dangerous Duo" by Maximilian Wechsler, in the *Bangkok Post*, July 6, 2008. Wechsler's article also mentions an underground facility, owned by Wei, at Pang Poi southwest of Panghsang, which is also allegedly used by Bang Ron, alias Surachai Ngernthongfu. However, Wechsler's information differs somewhat from what the authors understand. For instance, Wechsler states that Wei was born in 1952. That is the date of birth according to his now revoked Thai citizenship papers. In reality, he was born in 1946. Wechsler also states that Wei and Bang Ron "maintain contact with the outside world with mobile, satellite and land phones." According to other sources close to Wei, for security reasons he never uses mobile phones to conduct business. He has his messages hand-delivered to whoever he wants to convey orders or information of a personal or business-related nature. The quote from Colonel Kyaw Thein comes from "Thailand Worried About Relocation of Myanmar Minority," *Kyodo News Agency*, Bangkok, March 1, 2000. The BBC report can be viewed at http://news.bbc.co.uk/2/hi/asia-pacific/804326.stm. Personal details about Wei Xuegang were provided by confidential sources. For an account of the assassination of Sai Pao, see Bruce Hawke, "Burma's Ceasefire Agreements in Danger of Unraveling," *Jane's Intelligence Review*, November 1998. The *Time* cover story was called "Speed Tribe: Inside the World of the Wa—Asia's Deadliest Drug Cartel," which appeared in the December 16, 2002, edition. Details about the personal lives of the Bao brothers have been compiled from interviews with some of their associates, and Thai and Western narcotics intelligence reports. Bao Youxiang's favorite nephew, who is in charge of Nam Teuk, is called Ta Ai Roong. Xiao Minliang is quoted in Tom Kramer, *The United Wa State Party: Narco-Army or Ethnic Nationalist Party?* Policy Studies [Southeast Asia], no. 38 (Washington: East-West Center, 2007), 26. The five hundred kilograms of heroin (the actual figure was 496 kilograms) were seized from a convoy led by another of Bao Youxiang's nephews, Ta Ai Pan, or Ta Aik Pan. Charges were brought against him as an individual rather than against the UWSA as an organization—just another example of the benefits of the cease-fire agreement with the government. However, the seizure that occurred after the opium ban came into effect in the UWSA area was a hugely embarrassing to the Wa leadership, especially since the main culprit was a close relative of Ban Youxiang. In order to avoid a similar repeat of events, it was decided that the drug trade would from then on be more closely supervised by an inner committee of UWSA leaders. That move could also be seen to reflect a move to consolidate control over much needed revenues earned from the trade in advent of the financial constraints endured by Panghsang since the imposition of the 2005 opium ban. Details about the Red Guards in the Communist Party of Burma come from former party members who remember them well. One of the authors of this book has also interviewed all three of them: Lin Mingxian, Li Ziru, and Zhang Zhiming. One of the authors of this book met and talked to the CBS team before and after their trip to Burma in 1994. They also showed him their tapes from the visit. Also note that US Congressman Charles Rangel visited Rangoon in January 1988—a few months before the upheaval and massacres of that year—and then praised the government's anti-drug efforts. He also said that the Burmese army's war on drugs was a war not only for the Burmese people but also for the entire international community. The picture of Lin Mingxian and the Chinese ambassador to Rangoon appeared in the *Working People's Daily* of May 7, 1991. The overview of Lin Mingxian's business activities and connections today comes from firsthand sources in the area, but they cannot be named because it could cost them their lives. Data about Yawt Seik and other players on the Thai border also come from firsthand accounts, including interviews with several people close to the main players in the Golden Triangle. The attack on the Chinese patrol boat on the Mekong River, and Naw Kham's suspected involvement, was reported by the *Irrawaddy* and available online at http://www.irrawaddy.org/article.php?art_id=10624.

CHAPTER FIVE

For the news release from the DEA about the indictments, see http://www.usdoj. gov/dea/pubs/states/newsrel/nyc12505.html. See also the news release by the US DEA of January 25, 2005, "Eight High-Ranking Leaders of Southeast Asia's Largest Narcotics Trafficking Organization Indicted by a Federal Grand Jury in Brooklyn, New York." The *Time* cover story appeared on December 16, 2002. The UNODC's country profile for Burma can be viewed online at www.unodc.org/pdf/myanmar/ myanmar_country_profile_2005.pdf. The claim that there is very little violent crime and rape in Burma appears on page 27. For UN reports on human rights abuses in Burma, see http://www.burmalibrary.org/show.php?cat=932&lo=t&sl=0. Quotes from villagers in Shan State, the retired Burmese army officer, and Major General Thein Sein are from are from "Hand in Glove: The Burma Army and the Drug Trade in Burma," Shan Herald Agency for News, Chiang Mai, 2005. The openDemocracy website is at http://www.opendemocracy.net/democracy-protest/burma_4084.jsp, and the YouTube wedding clip can be found at http://www.youtube.com/watch? v=s6YPsycc6Lc. For the funding of Than Shwe's daughter's wedding, see http://www. irrawaddy.org/article.php?art_id=5597&page=6. The *Myanmar Times* article about Hong Pang can be viewed at http://www.myanmar.gov.mm/myanmartimes/no82/ myanmartimes5-82/News/6.htm. Colonel Hkam Awng is quoted in Tom Kramer, *The United Wa State Party: Narco-Army or Ethnic Nationalist Party?* Policy Studies 38, Southeast Asia (Washington: East-West Center 2007): 27. For the full text of Ko-lin Chin's and Sheldon X. Zhang's paper, see www.ncjrs.gov/pdffiles1/nij/grants/218254. pdf. Quotes from Jeremy Milsom are in Martin Jelsma, Tom Kramer, and Pietje Vervest (eds.), *Trouble in the Triangle: Opium and Conflict in Burma* (Chiang Mai: Silkworm Books, 2005), 75–75. Pasuk Phongpauchit's and Sungsidh Piriyarangsan's book is called *Corruption & Democracy in Thailand* (Chiang Mai, Silkworms Books, 2005). Another book that deals with corruption and the underground economy in

Thailand is Pasuk Phongpaichit, Sungsidh Piriyarangsan, and Nualnoi Treerat, *Guns, Girls, Gambling, Ganja: Thailand's Illegal Economy and Public Policy* (Chiang Mai: Silkworm Books, 1998). The *Caravan* article appeared in the August 1994 issue of the now defunct magazine. The report of the warrant for the arrest of a senior police officer appeared in the *Bangkok Post* of March 17, 1999. The report of arrests and dismissals of police officers in the wake of Bang Ron's escape appeared in Surat Jinakul, "Friends in High Places: Wealthy, well-connected and one step ahead of the law, illegal drug traffickers are cashing in on a booming trade," *Bangkok Post*, November 29, 1998. The *Bangkok Post* also reported on Justice Minister Pongthep Thepkanjana's request to find Bang Ron in Burma on July 24, 2003, but to no avail. The Burmese said they did not know where Wei was and they kept silent on Bang Ron. For the extradition of Li Yun-chung, see Bertil Lintner and Rodney Tasker, "Caged but Dangerous," *Far Eastern Economic Review*, June 5, 1997. For the arrest of Liu Wei Ming, see the *Bangkok Post* of April 1, 1997. A copy of the Möng La newspaper *Satalait*, or "Starlight," of August 1, 1995, is in the authors' possession. Information about Liu's involvement in the production of *ya-ee* was provided by drug enforcement officials in Chiang Mai, northern Thailand, and by local sources in the area. The Wa leader who claims the UWSA is no longer in the drug trade is quoted in Tom Kramer, *United Wa State Party*, 26. The full text of "The Bondage of Opium: The Agony of the Wa People, a Proposal and a Plea," is available online at http://www.burmalibrary.org/docs/BONDAGE.htm. One of the authors of this book met and interviewed Saw Lu in Chiang Mai in May 1993. For heroin seizures in China in 2006, see http://hong-kong.usconsulate.gov/uscn_narcos_2008022901.html.

CHAPTER SIX

For the creation of the Boten Border Trade Area, see "Placing Bets on Luang Nam Tha," *Bangkok Post*, April 13, 2008, a report confirmed by personal observations at the location. Information about Lin Mingxian's involvement in the Boten project comes from local sources in the area. For the announcement by the US Department of the Treasury, see www.fincen.gov/burma.pdf and www.fincen.gov/mayflowerbank.pdf. The ALTSEAN report was published on May 31, 2005, and titled "Call for FATF [Financial Action Task Force] to maintain Burma's NCCT [Non-Cooperative Country or Territory] status." The quote from the 2007

International Narcotics Control Strategy Report appeared on page 120. For gem business in Burma, see http://www.allmyanmar.com/new%20allmyanmar.com/ myanmar%20jade.htm. News about the arrival of Wei Xuegang and 300–350 Wa soldiers at Myawaddy was reported in the *Bangkok Post* of October 31, 1999. At the time, one of the authors of this book also received a detailed report from a local source about Wei's new enterprises in Myawaddy. For details about drug-related companies in Burma and the "whitening tax," see Anthony Davis and Bruce Hawke, "On the Road to Ruin: Narco-Dollars lure Burmese Junta toward Heroin Dependency," *Jane's Intelligence Review*, March 1998. See also "Burmese Tycoons," *Irrawaddy*, July 2000. Original company documents for Asia World are in the authors' possession. The interview with Khun Sa in Rangoon was published in the Austrian newspaper *Die Presse* on April 28, 1997, and July 30, 1997. The activities of the Shan State South Company were described in "Drug-linked Shan State Company Raking in Money," *Bangkok Post*, August 15, 2000. For details about Lin Mingxian's businesses, see "Lord of Burma's Mekong" in *Undercurrents: Monitoring Development on Burma's Mekong* (The Lahu National Development Organization, January 2005), 9–10. Planning minister Soe Tha was quoted by Agence France-Presse in Rangoon, May 25, 2008. For a detailed account of the demonstrations in September 2007, see "Burma: Crackdown, Repression of the 2007 Popular Protests in Burma" *Human Rights Watch*, December 2007, and *Bullets in the Alms Bowls: An Analysis of the Brutal SPDC Suppression of the September 2007 Saffron Revolution* (Human Rights Documentation Unit, National Coalition Government of the Union of Burma, March 2008). For the February 25, 2008, statement by the US Department of the Treasury, see "Burma: US Expands Sanctions Against Junta Supporters," Inter Press Service News Agency (Washington), February 25, 2008. For George W. Bush's statement, see "More Junta Cronies Hit by US Sanctions," *Irrawaddy*, February 26 2008. For regime cronies winning contracts to rebuild the delta, see *Irrawaddy*, May 16, 2008.

CHAPTER SEVEN

The best explanation of the difference between *bama* and *myanma* is found in the old Hobson-Jobson Dictionary, which despite its rather unorthodox name remains a very useful source of information: "The name (Burma) is taken from *Mran-ma*, the national name of the Burmese people, which they themselves generally pronounce *Bam-ma*, unless speaking formally and empathically." Both names have been used interchangeably throughout history, with Burma being the more colloquial name and Myanma or Myanmar a more formal designation, somewhat similar to Muang Thai and Prathet Thai in Thai. If Burma meant only the central plains and Myanmar the Burmese and all the other nationalities, how could there be, according the Myanmar Language Commission, a "Myanmar language"? The Commission's latest *Myanmar-English Dictionary* (1993) also mentions a "Myanmar alphabet." Clearly, Burma and Myanmar (and Burmese and Myanmar) mean exactly the same thing, and it cannot be argued that the term "Myanmar" includes any more people within the present union than the name "Burma" does. But the confusion is an old one and when the Burmese independence movement was established in the 1930s, there was a debate among the young nationalists as to what name should be used for the country: *bama* or *myanma*. The nationalists decided to call their movement the *Doh-bama Asiayone* ("Our Burma Association") instead of the Doh-myanma Asiayone. The reason, they said, was that "since the *doh-bama* was set up, the nationalists always paid attention to the unity of all the nationalities of the country . . . and the *thakins* (Burmese nationalists) noted that *myanma* meant only the part of the country where the myanma people lived. This was the name given by the Burmese kings to their country. *Bama naing-ngan* is not the country where only the *myanma* people live. Many different nationalities live in this country, such as the Kachins, Karens, Kayahs, Chins, P-Os, Palaungs, Mons, Myanmars, Rakhines, and Shans. Therefore, the nationalists did not use the term *myanma naing-ngan* but *bama naing-ngan*. That would be the correct term . . . all nationalities who live in *bama naing-ngan* are called *bama*." Thus, the movement became the *Doh-bama Asiayone* and not the *Doh-myanma Asiayone*. See "A Brief History of the *Doh-bama Asiayone*," an official government publication published in Burmese in Rangoon in 1976. The Burmese edition of the *Guardian* monthly, another official publication, also concluded in February 1971 that "the word *myanma* signifies only the *myanmars* whereas *bama* embraces all indigenous nationalities." In 1989, however, the present government decided that the opposite was true, and it is that view which many foreigners keep on repeating. The sad truth is that there is no term in Burmese or in any other language that covers both the *bama/myanma* and the ethnic minorities, since no such entity existed before the arrival of the British. Burma with its present boundaries is a creation of British colonialism, and successive governments of independent Burma have inherited a chaotic entity that is still struggling to find a common identity. But insisting that *myanma* means the whole country and in some way is a more indigenous term than *bama* is nonsense. Rangoon or Yangon is another reflection of the same kind of misunderstanding. Rangoon begins with the consonant *ra gaut*, or *r*, not *ya palait* or *y*. In English texts, Rangoon is therefore a more correct spelling. The problem is that the old *r* sound has died out in most Burmese dialects (although not in Arakanese and Tavoyan, which both have a very distinct *r* sound) and softened to a *y* sound in the same way as *r* often becomes *l* in Thai. The usage of "Yangon" is as childish as if the Thais insisted that Ratchaburi had to be spelt "Latbuli" in English, or that Buriram should be Bulilam. See also Bertil Lintner, "Cultural Revolution," *Far Eastern Economic Review*, November 18, 1999. For the reference to the "myanmafication of Burma," see Gustaaf Houtman, *Mental Culture in Burmese Crisis Politics: Aung San Suu Kyi and the National League for Democracy* (Tokyo: Institute for the Study of Languages and Cultures of Asia and Africa, Tokyo University of Foreign Studies, 1999). The quote from Than Shwe's speech of March 27, 2006, comes from *Irrawaddy*, April 2006. We have changed the *Irrawaddy*'s spelling of the names of the kings in line with the standard form of romanization. For the statement by the Human Rights Watch, see http://www. hrw.org/reports/2008/burma0508/4.htm. The article "Wa and Peace: The UWSA and tensions in Myanmar," which appeared in the March 2008 issue of *Jane's Intelligence Review*, was written by Michael Black and Anthony Davis, and based on interviews with local sources in the area. For Chinese arms in the hands of rebels in northeastern India, see "Chinese arms best choice for North-east rebel outfits," *Sentinel*, June 24, 2008. The article by the critical Indian writer, Satya Sagar, can be viewed at http://zcommunications.org/znet/viewArticle/14333. The quote from Hudeyuki Takano is taken from *Time* (Asia), December 16, 2002. See also his book *The Shore Beyond Good and Evil: A Report from Inside Burma's Opium Kingdom* (Tokyo: Kotan Publishing, 2002). The Human Rights Watch reports are *My Gun Was as Tall as Me: Child Soldiers in Burma* (October 2002) and *Sold to be Soldiers: The Recruitment and Use of Child Soldiers in Burma* (October 2007). The Burmese drug report is titled *2006 Annual report of the Drug Abuse Collection Network Myanmar* and was compiled by Dr. Gyaw Htet Doe. The quote from Xavier Bouan is at http://www.atimes.com/atimes/Southeast_Asia/IJ23Ae01.html. For the full texts of the 1973 and 1975 proposals to terminate the opium trade in

Shan State, as well as the US State Department's response, see Bertil Lintner, "The Shans and the Shan State of Burma," *Contemporary Southeast Asia*, March 1984. The US General Accounting Office's report was released in September 1989 and titled *Drug Control Enforcement Efforts in Burma Are Not Effective* (GAO/NSIAD-89-197.) A copy of the NLD's 1989 manifesto is in the authors' possession.

INDEX